How NOT to Be a Perfect Famil

Libby Purves was a late s
at thirty-two. However, t
accumulate some useful e
barmaid, broadcaster, tra
the editor – for six excitin society
magazine *Tatler*. This career gave her a valuable grounding in the motherly arts of pacifying unreasonable individuals, managing without sleep, and being able to talk her way out of trouble. In 1986, with children aged two and three, she was so exasperated by the perfectionist tone of other child-care books that she wrote the much-loved *How Not to Be a Perfect Mother*. In 1988 she and her husband, Paul Heiney, set out to sail 1700 miles round Britain in their small boat with children of three and five. She published the story in *One Summer's Grace* in 1990. This was followed by *How Not to Raise a Perfect Child* (three- to eight-year-olds) in 1991.

She lives in Suffolk with her husband and children (now aged nine and eleven) on a small farm, travels to London once a week to present the Radio 4 programme 'Midweek', and writes for *The Times* and other newspapers and magazines.

Also by Libby Purves

Britain at Play
How Not to Be a Perfect Mother
The Sailing Weekend Book (*with Paul Heiney*)
One Summer's Grace
How Not to Raise a Perfect Child

How NOT to Be a Perfect Family

Libby Purves

Drawings by Viv Quillin

HarperCollins*Publishers*

HarperCollins*Publishers*
77–85 Fulham Palace Road
Hammersmith, London W6 8JB
A Paperback Original 1994
9 8 7 6 5 4 3 2 1

A catalogue record for this book
is available from the British Library

ISBN 0 00 638121 9

Set in Linotron Palatino by
Rowland Phototypesetting Ltd,
Bury St Edmunds, Suffolk

Printed in Great Britain by
HarperCollinsManufacturing Glasgow

To Nicholas and Rose, for putting up with it all

Contents

Foreword and Forewarning

This is a very presumptuous book, and having a wholesome dread of anything that looks like a self-help manual, I would not have written it if I had not been urged to, jointly and severally, by people of strong will and persuasive manner. Nor would I dare to put forward any personal views on family life if a number of newspapers and magazines had not, over the preceding decade, actively (sometimes bullyingly) solicited me to. So I am grateful to them, particularly *The Times*, *She*, and *Good Housekeeping*, for their always thoughtful commissioning discussions, on which parts of this book have been based; and also to my agent, Lisa Eveleigh, and publisher, Lucinda McNeile, for their dogged insistence that I write it.

However, none of them should be held responsible for the content of the following pages. It is in many ways highly erratic. Being heartily sick of reading psychobabble and anxious treatises on parenting, which arrive on the female freelance journalist's desk by every single post, I have sometimes found that in sheer reaction I have covered in two brusque paragraphs a subject which elsewhere occupies whole shelves in the public library. That is my decision. On the other hand, I also seem at times to have veered wildly off at great length into autobiography, or gossip about other families; or gone on for pages and pages about some triviality which seems to have taken over all my attention for weeks.

But that is family life for you: unbalanced, unplannable, seat-of-the-pants navigation without instruments or charts. The family is an oddly designed and unpredictable vessel: push the tiller one way and it may veer the other; it may sail through crisis and near-bankruptcy without trouble, only to pile up on the rocks of a bad attack of constipation or a daughter's unsavoury boyfriend.

What is more, no two families are alike in more than a few ways: advice or anecdotes which hit the button for one family may seem utterly louche and baffling to another. So, come to think of it, it would have been more of an insult to the subject to write a structured textbook on it. Or so I tell myself.

Anyway, feel free to disagree. And to laugh, even at the bits which I never intended to be funny.

1: Who Needs the Family, Anyway?

Oh dear, oh dear: why write about family life? Especially, why try to prescribe anything useful about how to lead it?

In this century the whole subject has become a snake-pit, a hissing confusion of opinion and bigotry and sentimentality. There was a time when everyone more or less knew what a family was, and said nothing about it that you couldn't embroider on a sampler, as in *Blood is thicker than water*, or *A boy's best friend is his mother*; or at worst, *Good breeding always tells*. Then came voices of dissent, going along with Philip Larkin's dictum that *They f—— you up, your Mum and Dad; they may not mean to, but they do. They give you all the faults they had and add some extra, just for you*. Freud didn't help much, either, with his gloomy theories about how easy it is to mess up a small child's mind for life. The hippy Sixties drugged us into a vague idea that all mankind was our family – with the possible exception of our real family, who were extremely uncool and laid a heavy guilt trip on us, man, and put the mockers on drugs and group sex. Then the politicians got hold of the family as a wonderful scapegoat for everything they couldn't, or wouldn't, attempt to cure by public policy, and family values were chattered about by peacock-vain male politicians who spent their days plotting in corridors and their afternoons in bed with their secretaries, and rarely went near an actual child. (In the House of Commons, there was at one stage a Standing Committee on the Family which met at five-thirty: precisely the time, as Harriet Harman MP used to point out acidly, when anyone who had anything to do with a real family was busy getting tea and baths and homework sorted out.)

So we reach a point where every time anybody says anything on the subject, half a dozen rival pundits leap down his throat.

Family Life is in decline! Oh no, it isn't, it's just changing! I blame the selfish parents! I blame society! Kids today, what do they know? Spoilt, the lot of them! Divorce should be banned! No, it should be easier! Child poverty is a scandal in an affluent society/all the fault of the parents/much exaggerated/a hidden scourge . . . Why any sane woman should want to raise her head above the parapet and join in this argument is a mystery. Even to me.

But families are the cornerstone of life. No point trying to dodge round it, or theorize about how it might be in a Utopian kibbutz or free society where child care was communal; the fact is that when the chips are down, everyone needs a mother, or father. Or son or daughter; or sister, brother, cousin, uncle, granny. Someone who is bound to you by blood, by early memory, by habitual – even if grudging and flawed – affection. As Robert Frost said, 'Home is the place where, when you have to go there, they have to take you in'. Family are the people who, when nobody else does, have to care.

And they do. Even the lousiest families count for something; and most families are not lousy at all, but something bordering on heroic. Parents cope with incredible burdens, as do grown-up children of the old and helpless, and quietly self-sacrificing relatives who stop the weakest in society from going all the way to the wall. The fact that we are shocked by – and heavily publicize – family breakdown is only proof of how strong the institution still is, and how much we expect from it.

But we cannot look at the family clearly. The waters have been muddied by too much public posturing. All over Europe, particularly in Britain, strident political voices spent the 1980s and early 90s decrying the decline of the traditional family. They wring their hands over divorce and over co-habitation without marriage, write off every unmarried couple as irresponsible flower-children and every divorced one as vicious and selfish. They constantly appeal to nebulous, never-quite-determined 'family values', and blame the absence of old-fashioned family life for everything from football violence to child abuse. They say that the bourgeois family has been a king plank in the construction of Western civilization, and that we ignore its role at our peril. They wring their hands over modern habits like television-watching and the replacement of family meals by 'grazing'; they mourn each year's new statistics showing that, actually, only one household in four consists of two parents and dependent children, and that one in four of those will end up divorced anyway. They forecast general social collapse, with no real cure in sight (after all, what are you going to do about this state of affairs? Pass a law saying divorcees must get back together instantly? Make family Sunday lunch compulsory?).

Rarely, however, have these prophets of doom defined precisely which traditional family values they wanted to keep. They talked of authority, but forgot the stifling days of 'Mother Knows Best', and 'Wait Until Your Father Gets Home'. They talked of idyllic homes, symmetrical and conventional, providing loving firmness and a secure base, but forgot the tyrannies and constraints of much traditional family life, and the way that creative or enterprising children have, down the years, often fled from it for their very survival. They ignored loving and balanced households which did not fit the norm of two-married-parents-and-natural-children, pointing instead at the poor, the desperate, the dangerously uneducated and mentally subnormal

homes where children were, indeed, often in grave danger.

These traditional-family enthusiasts would notice 'normal' (i.e. symmetrical and nuclear) families which were happy, handsome and prosperous. They deified them in a thousand glutinous magazine profiles, making it seem as if the pattern of Mum-Dad-and-two-kids was somehow a guarantee of happiness. Rarely did they focus on those families which, despite their marriage lines and outward conventionality, were quite dreadful. Every bit as dreadful, in fact, as their bugbear, the terminally unconventional Mia Farrow–Woody Allen type of household. Too many critics ignored the fact that conventional families can be abusive, mean and sour and restrictive and drive their children to drugs or delinquency. When the Mothers' Union in Britain, bastion of conventionality and Christian values, published a controversial view in 1993 casting doubt on the happiness of small, tight nuclear families, and asking whether the extended family was not more worth focusing on, there were hostile snorts of 'trendy' and 'disgraceful', and few commentators dared show any sympathy.

It is a pity, because many of the points being made by fans of the nuclear family are valid, and many of their trendier, hippyish opponents who dislike the very idea of family have missed the point. They throw out the baby with the bath water. Truth lies somewhere in between: for instance, while it is true that you don't need a gold wedding ring to give a child security, it is equally true that a rapidly changing procession of 'stepfathers' doesn't help much either. 'Free love', advocated by 'free spirits', is a lousy environment in which to bring up children. Or again, it is true that certain social policies directly threaten the traditional family; but those policies are rarely intended to do so, and often come from the most traditionalist governments. The Thatcher government in Britain spoke constantly and hectoringly about family values; but many of its policies disastrously undermined family budgets. For a long time, for example, in terms of tax and mortgage relief, cohabitation was more sensible and economical than marriage for any young working couple in Britain. Never has any British government made child care tax-deductible for working mothers (although black trousers worn by barristers are!). And all over Europe, the design of housing estates and urban traffic plans from the 1950s onwards has contributed, very powerfully indeed, to making the business of staying at home rearing children as miserable as possible. The streets where once children played, the safe parks, the communal facilities have tended to be run down. And where community life collapses, families too collapse: because in a perfectly balanced society, the community supports and indeed improves the family. The playground, the village hall, the pub, the friendly clinic, the safe park are as important in the life of a happy family as its own hearth.

Well, we let community life slide, and now, as in America, the hateful concept of 'cocooning', a perversion of family life, is gaining favour. In 'cocooning', the nuclear family hides in its own prissy little bunker, watching videos with the burglar alarm set, and refuses to engage with the outside world – certainly not with other people's nasty rough children and potentially dangerous teenagers. The cocoon, chill and mean and hostile to community life, is one of the worst starts any child can have; but whenever a freakish incident like the murder of Jamie Bulger in Liverpool by ten-year-old children occurs, one can sense a whole nation drawing its children closer to its skirts and banging the front door on society.

Somewhere in the middle of all this public hysteria, the ordinary family – not extremists, not cocooners, not too concerned with abstract moral questions or Utopian social policies – tries to muddle along. Parents get by, often without very much sleep for several years, trying to run the home according to general principles of decency and fairness, and half-remembered maxims from their own parents who lived in another age. Not much help is at hand: economics dictate that a lot of mothers who hate working full-time have to do so; advertisers constantly throw images of perfection at us from the TV fantasy world when we are too tired and demoralized even to push aside the child's sweater whose sleeve is hanging down, dirty, over the screen. Politicians lecture us (especially mothers) on our duties, while national policies on working mothers, tax, child care and education alter bewilderingly every few years just to keep the goal posts moving.

Even the rise of self-understanding and therapeutic psychobabble – which could have helped – has not always been entirely useful. Psychologists tell us such alarming things about the ill-effects of 'dysfunctional' families that it is easy to become paralysed with indecision over the simplest moments of family life. In one interview I did for a newspaper I was bombarded with case histories from psychiatrists' consulting rooms: by the time I had heard about a woman who had disastrous affairs because her father was too possessive, teenagers with eating disorders caused by their fathers not caring enough (tricky to hit that medium, chaps, but keep trying), and men whose impotence was caused by their mothers going to work – Aaaargh! – I hardly dared go home and put the fish fingers under the grill for fear of what I was storing up for my children.

That is not what this book is about. It contains few theories, few prescriptions. It is more of an imperfectionist paean to the great art of muddling-through and the great quality of common sense and looking steadily at what is right in front of your nose. Not all the common sense is originally mine, since I have been as prone to daft prejudices down the years as anybody. Some of what I am going to say will strike a lot of readers as being what Basil Fawlty would call 'Glimpses of the Bleeding Obvious'; but all the signposts are ones which, in moments of tearfulness, doubt, fury, resentment and 'flu, I have at times lost sight of myself. Everything is tried and tested, even if only by mistake. Everything is, in the final analysis, perfectly simple – glimpses of the obvious: be kind, be fair, be forgiving – but be those things to yourself, as well as everybody else.

As we muddle through, though, we ought to acknowledge a deep, inescapable truth: that the family, like every social institution, has to renew and re-invent itself all the time. Otherwise, it is nothing but a fossilized habit, a superstition as meaningless as throwing salt over your shoulder to spite the devil. So through divorce, bereavement, trauma, bankruptcy, disablement, confusion and irregularity, what each of us has to do is focus on the reality of our own family, as it is. Be free, be inventive, follow your best instincts; think of kindness before fairness, and fairness before convenience; and if the result looks odd to the neighbours, then to hell with them. No two families are entirely alike, and there is little point looking for example to the one next door, or the one in the TV sitcom, or, God forbid, advertisement. Look at your own. Most of this book presumes a more or less conventional family with two adults of opposite sexes, and dependent children, but a remarkable number of the same principles apply to other kinds of family, because any family, even if fatherless, motherless, or plain weird, is a marvellous organism in its own right.

And it has got to be. Whether warm and secure or draughty and defective, the family is the only nest your fledglings have got; in its depths, squabbling cosily, they grow. And you grow, too. And eventually the fledglings reach their teens and can see clearly over the side: they spread their wings, and struggle free, and with luck they start to fly. The great merit of a good family is that it enables individuals to fly freely from it, confident and alone and unfettered. Fit to start another family, and pass on happiness and strength down the generations.

2: Becoming a Family

'Aaaah!' the old ladies say, leaning over you in the maternity ward, more often than not breathing sherry fumes from an outbreak of family celebration. 'You're a lovely little family now!' This makes couples feel rather strange, as if the only thing that anchors them as a unit in society is the whiffling baby in the transparent cot. It seems to act like a sort of scrunched-up, squidgy national identity card. A ticket of entrance to the theme park called Familyland. Even stranger is the thought that you have become 'A Family' instead of a couple; and that you will never be just a couple again.

But of course it does not actually happen all at once. There is no such thing as an instant family (as many step-parents can tell you, with grimaces). Why should there be? You cannot make an instant garden or an instant farm, and a family is every bit as complex, organic and prone to blight.

What we have in the twentieth-century Western world is often a very gradual transition from singlehood into family life. Instead of an abrupt step, now that so many couples live together outside wedlock, a curiously gentle slope has been created from bachelorhood to marriage. No longer are you expected to cope with your first house, first sex, first taste of living with someone who isn't a relation, and first pregnancy all in one go. God knows how anybody ever survived it. Today, in most cases, the slope is gentler: you date, you start staying in instead of going out, one of you cooks for the other; you decide you might as well share a flat and save the bus fares. If you get on well together you may get married. Then, unless you are hellbent on an early baby, you carry on much as before. A couple, but not a family: affectionate and committed flat mates, but each with your separate job and a few separate friends and interests.

Of course, you each came from a family of your own. They are likely to be rather shadowy at this point, and a good thing too. Husbands and wives who run home to mother for a bit of decent cooking and sympathy are not concentrating on the job in hand. It is necessary for new couples to be just that: Adam and Eve, starting the world together. That is the only sensible preparation for the responsibility of parenthood. During early couplehood, wise parents of adults keep their distance, offer their support only if needed, and generally cool down their natural parental ardour. Their time will come again. As grand-parents.

Because if the idea of 'family' fades away a little when you are courting, it returns in a new, bewildering, joyful and terrifying form when the first baby comes. I have written enough about the nuts and bolts of this enormous, shattering change (in *How Not to Be a Perfect Mother*) but what was not as clear to me then as it is now, eight years on, is that when you first have a baby you really have hardly any grasp of what is waiting for you in terms of family life. In fact, if the mother goes back to work after maternity leave, you are quite likely to end up behaving like the bachelor-couple you were, only with an obstacle course to get round. The baby becomes another management problem in a crowded modern life. 'If you've got a ten o'clock meeting, you could drop James at the childminder and pick up the dry-cleaning, then I could get to my appointment early enough to nip into the shops for more nappies and some supper. If I could have the car, because of the dentist afterwards . . .'

This causes much wear and tear on the parents, especially if the mother works in the kind of office where everyone gaily pretends that nothing much changes when you have a child; but the new baby knows no better, and as long as it is warm and fed and cuddled a lot by someone, it generally puts up with the situation and thrives.

And gets bigger. And starts getting firm, outspoken preferences about its minders, parents, meal-times, and sleeping habits. By the time a baby is two, there is no disguising the fact that you are turning into a three-cornered unit: a family. Instead of a strong adult couple protecting a weak, helpless scrap of life and making bossy decisions about every aspect of its routine, you have three strong wills. All trying to inhabit the same space. Fraser Harrison, author of *A Winter's Tale*, the story of a temporary family crisis, described it beautifully as feeling as if you were all sewn into the same small suit, struggling to find space, or indeed a sleeve-hole.

It is not uncommon for the two-year-old to have the strongest personality in the house, and for parents to feel they are struggling feebly for survival themselves. Every parent of a toddler should give themselves an undemanding evening sometime by watching the hit Disney film *Honey I Blew Up the Kid*. I found myself riveted with fascination by this sci-fi fantasy, early on when the toddling baby grows to seven feet tall and starts lurching around the house, ripping off doors and causing chaos. Surreal as this sequence was, it rang horribly true: there are times when the presence of a toddler is the largest thing in the house, and everything hangs from his or her whim. I spent the rest of the film – while the baby stumps around Los Angeles like a capricious King Kong – brooding on this, only to find myself nodding wisely, deeply moved, when it reached its denouement. The solution, you will remember, is that Mommy has to become even bigger than the child in order to reassert organization and peace. 'Gee,' I said, Disneyishly. 'That is so true. A Mommy has gotta be bigger, in every way, than her kid.'

If one parent has stayed at home full-time, the process of becoming a three-cornered family happens slightly faster, but more unevenly, usually precipitated by the mother deciding to bark a few home truths at the insouciant homecoming father, along the lines of 'I don't care what sort of a day you've had, I haven't had time even to look at the paper, have you any idea how much work a baby is?' Either way, gradually a family emerges. If more children follow the first, the mixture becomes richer and more complex, the juggling and compromising more skilled. A family is growing, a team is building up. There is not a lot you can do with the individual building-blocks, but all of

you somehow have to fit together into a viable structure: the egotist, the nervy one, the martyr, the short fuse. The family becomes an organism, so that it is impossible to imagine life outside it. One day, the parents look in an old diary or photograph album and say 'Good Heavens! There really was, once long ago, a time when we had nothing to do but earn a living and keep ourselves amused! What did we do all day?' In the grip of this new job, the family job, they can hardly believe it was ever so simple.

So let the family grow, gently, at its own pace. Don't look at other families and say 'Oh, they're so happy, they do so much together, it's all so well run and harmonious'. It probably isn't, once the front door is shut. Look instead at what is nearest: the state of mind and happiness of your own children.

And one another. At the heart of the family there is the marriage. *Un homme et une femme*. It is amazing how often this gets forgotten about, in the general chaos of family life, family rows, meals, dilemmas about school, desperate dawn searches for Cub woggles and lost homework, confrontations with sullen teenagers and sleepless nights with sick babies. But we forget at our peril that there's still a marriage in there somewhere. If there had never been attraction, flirtation, love and passion then there would be no family. For the physical passion to cool down for a while is quite understandable (hell, what better contraceptive could there be than a new baby?), but even that will, with luck and humour, come back. Because if the love and attraction and mutual amusement and appreciation in a marriage go sour, there will be estrangement. And separation. And divorce.

And – let us not mince matters – unhappy children. There was a period in the Sixties and Seventies when it was fashionable to pretend that children really didn't mind divorce and that they preferred their parents to be happy and 'fulfilled'. More recent, and more honest, investigation has confirmed what most of us knew by instinct anyway: that short of real violence, children prefer almost anything to the break-up of the familiar family. They do not like having their loyalties divided, hate the artificiality of access arrangements, and secretly blame themselves for it having happened. For a child, its parents' 'emotional fulfilment', like their professional fulfilment, is a pretty damn low priority (when did you last hear a child say 'Gosh, the best Christmas present I could get is for Mummy to get her promotion to Marketing Director – her career fulfilment is really important to me!' or 'I'm really pleased that Dad has found a woman who really understands him at last'?) This is perfectly fair: they didn't ask to be born. They didn't impose themselves on us. We invited them, and we owe them the basic courtesy of a secure home and access to their parents.

If divorce is inevitable, the plain duty of both parents is to bite the bullet, swallow their pride, and behave with impeccable good manners, fairness and consideration of the child's feelings. I drove a small boy home once to his mother's, after a weekend with his father and new girlfriend. In the car he said, 'I wish I hadn't had so much fun at the swimming pool.' Why? 'Because my Mum always asks me if I've had a nice time with Dad and Wendy, and if I say I have, she cries and says I like him best. But if I tell a lie and say I haven't had much fun, then I feel I'm being bad to him.' Dad, it must be said, had behaved pretty scummily towards this child's mother, but she had no right to pass on the pain. It was hers: part of her life's allocation of misery, not transferable. I could have throttled her. When we arrived she came to the door and hugged the boy and said, 'Did you have a nice time?' – and he said, 'Sort of,' and gave me a guilty glance. It was horrible.

Most parents behave a little better than that, and some with exemplary restraint and charity. Inevitably, doing this involves a certain amount of personal humiliation and a burning sense of unfairness in at least one party ('He's off with his girlfriend, buying them treats, I struggle through the school week, nurse them when they're ill . . .' 'She's got the house, the kids, her new man, I live in a crummy bedsit to pay the maintenance . . .'). But in the end, everybody will be happier if they have behaved well. And there is even a kind of justice at the last: children are not fools. As they grow older they will know which parent behaved best, and work out what it must have cost them.

But never mind divorce. Marriages can be kept in good repair, and once there are children involved, they ought to be.

3: *Un Homme et une Femme*: Marriage Maintenance

In 1837 the 28-year-old Charles Darwin scribbled out a list of pros and cons concerning marriage. In favour he found: 'Children (if it please God) – constant companion (friend in old age) who will feel interested in one, object to be beloved and played with – better than a dog anyhow – Home, and someone to take care of house – charms of music and female chit-chat. These things good for one's health. Forced to visit and receive relations but terrible waste of time.'

Further tormented, he moved to the advantages of not marrying. 'Not forced to visit relatives and to bend in every trifle – to have the expense and anxiety of children – perhaps quarrelling . . . less money for books etc.' He only stopped short of the brutal frankness of one relative of mine who dismisses the whole business of married life as 'Harsh words by day, foul smells by night'.

It may make us gasp, but such frankness with oneself before marriage is not at all a bad thing. Younger women in particular have a dreadful tendency to blind themselves to the realities of marriage, refusing to envisage the relentless daily companionship, the hairs in the washbasin, the real implications of 'in sickness and in health'. They allow a cloud of white tulle and rose petals to obscure such vital questions as, 'Does this man really just want someone to take care of him, "better than a dog anyhow", good for his health?' The American idea of a premarital contract laying out everything from finance to childbearing is perhaps taking it a bit far, but an astonishing number of engaged couples have never even discussed the possibility of children, let alone who is going to look after them. As for talking about such matters as who would be most likely to relocate across the country to follow whose career promotion, I have only ever met one couple who talked about it before the wedding. And they got divorced within two years.

But that private Darwinian list of pros and cons might be a useful thing to concentrate one's mind. The best bit of advice about marriage is 'Don't do it unless you can't bear not to'. And the best description of marriage is Robert Louis Stevenson's: 'Marriage is one long conversation, chequered by disputes. Two persons more and more adapt their notions one to suit the other, and in process of time, without sound of trumpet, they conduct each other into new worlds of thought.' Ergo, if you can't hold an enjoyable conversation with someone, and haven't adopted some of each other's thoughts, think twice about getting married. In the USA there are such people as 'predictive premarital counsellors' to help you, and one of the things they ask every engaged couple is, 'Imagine the marriage of the woman's mother to the man's father, and her father to his mother.' If it seems unthinkable, they reckon you should call it off. A bit extreme (yes, yes, I know, you have only just got up off the floor after hideous imaginings of your in-laws pairing off), but I suppose it works, up to a point. I mean, would the Queen of England have enjoyed being married to the explosive, oversexed, horsey Major Ron Ferguson? And did their children's marriage work? There you are, then. But perhaps it is best not to think about such things too carefully, or the human race would die out.

Once you do marry, no question about it: you feel different. I had only been ten days wed when I fell into bad company at an office party after my early morning radio news shift. It lasted all morning and developed into a pub lunch. I got home at about three o'clock, singing, and spent some time trying to get the key into the front door of the flat. Then I fell face downward on the bed and knew no more until I woke up in the chilly dusk and remembered that it had been my turn to take the communal pillowcase round to the laundrette. A fortnight earlier, living in the same flat with the same man and the same bag of shirts, I would have shrugged philosophically and left it for the morning. In my new status as a married lady I panicked. Too drunk to do the laundry! The sure mark of a Bad Wife! The shame of it! This was replaced later by a conviction that I was a Bad Mother (not cutting babies' nails often enough, putting them in non-matching booties) and a Bad Housekeeper (never any lavatory paper). Until one day I saw the light, and realized that wearing a white frilly dress for a couple of hours does not convert a slob into a *hausfrau*, and never was going to; any more than there is a magic spell in the wedding ceremony capable of turning a frog into a prince, or a roaring rugby fullback into a man whose greatest thrill is to trail round Habitat looking for rattan bathroom stools. *Caveat emptor*: if you don't like it, don't marry it. I saw that my husband married a person, not an idea; and that the only real essential was that we should carry on the conversation that we had started.

This is harder than it sounds. There is a mysterious process by which couples who, while courting, spend hours going on and on about their innermost souls, childhood memories and deepest aspirations, often find that after marriage the conversation dwindles down to 'Have you seen my hair dryer?' and 'We're supposed to be going to the Carters in half an hour, or was it yesterday?' By the time children arrive it can be a positive struggle even to get these simple messages across. I was once asked to write a Valentine poem for a newspaper's collection, and rather to my horror found that this came out:

Had we but world enough and time
This note would be a Valentine
Since married life is what we have
It's to remind you to bring home the haddock and the Sanilav.

But the real conversation must go on. Couples with children have different ways of seeing that it does so. Some go on holiday together without their children once a year. This is all very well, especially if you have a good Granny on duty, but it can backfire if you are a working mother who feels she spends little enough time with the children anyway or – like me – the kind of neurotic worrier who wastes the whole holiday worrying whether they are all right. I have traipsed round Venice sobbing, 'Gosh, the children would love this,' and that was only a weekend.

Weekends alone together, though, are good even for us neurotics: and it is amazing how much conversation (as well as drinking) you can fit in between Friday and Sunday evenings if you are without children or much other company. It may seem artificial to isolate yourselves as a couple, but it really does pay off. Formality can help: my husband and I both work mainly at home, although at very different occupations, and sometimes make an actual appointment to have lunch together while the children are at school. During the most tumultuous years of childrearing and keeping two careers going, we devised a habit of holding an Annual General Meeting on Boxing Day. We got in a babysitter, and walked off the Christmas festivities on an epic fifteen- or twenty-mile walk lasting all day. The purpose of this walk was to discuss the past year, how life had gone, and what we both really wanted to do next. If we could not afford lunch, or a babysitter, I suppose we would just announce one television-free evening a week when the children were in bed, and talk then. It may sound astonishingly simple and obvious, but it is quite clear to us that when we have spent too long a period not taking these deliberate chances to talk uninterrupted, we become angry and snappish and difficult. We lose communication.

Even if the conversations themselves are difficult (i.e., too much about money, or troublesome relatives) it is essential to have them. Otherwise a marriage slowly weakens like an unwatered plant, and falls prey to the first gale. And one says to the other 'I never knew you were feeling like that! I had no idea!' and the other says 'It's too late now!'

Through conversation, and frankness, and a willingness to admit to anger or irritation (over money, or sex, or working hours, or who gets up first, or the way you speak to one another in company), you get a better understanding of what the psychiatrist Robin Skynner calls the 'secret contracts' of marriage. Old idealisms about equality, openness, mutual respect and home-made bread give way to pragmatism and

an understanding of your real needs. As Skynner once said to me: 'People marry for some very obvious reasons and for others not obvious even to themselves. The businessman who seems powerful and strong, even to himself, marries a wife with a traditional submissive role; but there may be a secret contract that she will mother and nurture him. A downtrodden wife may be, secretly, the boss; a strong, decisive woman may want to be cosseted and tucked in at night. Just look at the Valentine columns in the papers, all that baby talk about Piggy-Wiggy and Snugglebotty. People get married because they want to be babies with each other sometimes. But that's not in the formal contract, is it? Although it's just as important.'

Sex

Sex, of course, is in the formal contract. 'With my body I thee worship.' The arrival of children changes all that. The female body, in particular, starts worshipping the idea of a quiet night's sleep, without anything crying or kicking and wriggling in the bed or needing its nappy changed. As long as both parents are utterly flattened by night cries and daily pacing, the problem is not too serious. But if Daddy is fresh as a daisy, and has not quite grasped his new status, he can become aggrieved. Women naturally become angry at being pressed; and men get angry too.

One friend of mine, Eric, otherwise as hip a New Man as you could ever hope to dodge in the supermarket before he told you about his wife's afterbirth, expressed his resentment in startlingly primitive terms. 'It's as if she'd got what she wanted out of me, and I was a redundant breeding animal.' Well, Eric, I said in my supportive way, that is exactly what you are, really, isn't it? Or did you want another baby on the anniversary? We then came to a more reasonable conversation about it, and concluded that the problem is that since the Pill we have separated pleasure and love too sharply from the bald biological *raison d'être* of sex. The result is that when children are born – baldly and biologically – we expect the pleasure to go on operating independently, as it did before. But Nature thinks otherwise, and little as new mothers are likely to admit it, she closes down the female libido with pragmatic ruthlessness during most of the lactation period.

This is not to say that breastfeeding women don't make love: it is a matter of the kind of love they make. If a woman has dwelt upon an erotic pedestal, and sex has hitherto been associated with clean tumbling hair, fresh nighties, candlelight and a crooner on the stereo, the contrast with the earthy chaos of early motherhood may be too much for both partners. If sex has been playfully and consentingly violent, things may have to change even more radically. Diana, a single girl reputed in hushed conversation to 'know all the tricks', eventually made a colourful marriage and spoke freely to the rest of us of vibrators, the old school gymslip and kinky whips. Then she turned up one day wild-eyed at a baby-circle coffee morning and said, 'I think I've gone frigid. Every time we try I keep thinking Hell, I'm not some tuppenny trollop, I'm a mother, I've got responsibilities, I'm not going to have him licking honey out of my navel!' Those of us who had always tended more towards cuddly, comforting couplings suddenly realized we were not such losers after all. The comforting cuddles never stop, the couplings just develop again when the time is ripe. Diana and her husband, in the end, seem to have discovered other depths to sex than mere gymnastics: years later she said to me that whereas some of their old fun and games had re-surfaced, all the oriental postures and kinky knickers in the world couldn't, in the end, match up to the extraordinary and mysterious knowledge that by doing this once before, you had created a miracle.

Even if you are doing your damnedest to stop another miracle happening just yet, that feeling remains: the marvel of Life trying to happen. And the extraordinary fact is that sex is actually better – if different – on the far side of childbirth. Men and women who understand this stay together. The ones who don't – the women who cool off entirely, or grant themselves grudgingly as a favour, the men who see no difference and grumble at the roundedness and tiredness of the maternal woman – are the ones who fall into the miserable chaos of affairs and estrangements. Take your pick. As in so many areas of family life, you can't have everything: but you can, with patience and humour, get a great deal of it.

Fighting

I sometimes think that TV drama must have had a disastrous effect on marriage. Not merely because it innocently gives the impression that all husbands and wives are attractive and have swish fitted kitchens, but because of the rows. Think of the last half-dozen plays (or even sitcoms) that you saw, and I bet there were at least six marital screaming matches. I also bet that five out of six of them ended in passionate embraces. The one that sticks in my mind is the infertility mini-series, *You, Me, and It*, in which a yuppie couple were unspeakably nasty to one another for months and we were expected to believe that the moment she got pregnant all the vile words would be forgotten. Hmmm.

I suppose that because of the demands of drama – hell, something has to happen, and insults are amusing to onlookers – writers have overdone the rows. Ever since Jimmy berated Alison for two hours in *Look Back in Anger* before turning back into her cuddly bear, there has been a dramatic convention that such rows do not damage the relationship but actually ginger it up. Parts of the therapy industry – and the feminist movement – now seem to be keenly bolstering this idea that people should 'express anger freely'. Take Dr Elizabeth Stanley, who recently said in a newspaper 'It may be that the couples who have the more open rows – the ones who appear to outsiders to have a dreadful marriage, always yelling at each other – may have a better, stronger relationship. Because anger, constructively expressed, will clear the air. If they say "we never argue", it rings warning bells.' Or another recent claim in a magazine that 'Couples who fight aren't strictly those who divorce the most. Lack of communication is more damaging than furious rows'.

Hmmm again. Of course there is something in that point of view: occasionally a row does clear the air, and the most poisonous marriages of all are undoubtedly the tight, bitter, silent ones. Many a woman has been frustrated by a man who refuses to join in arguments at all, merely retiring behind a newspaper in lofty silence while she smashes teapots. Angela, married ten years to Alan, walked out last summer citing the fact that whenever she raised any point he disagreed with 'he sort of sighs, and goes on with what he's doing, and doesn't answer'. Wives have been known to pull the same trick by merely bursting into tears instead of pursuing a discussion. It is perfectly true that a marriage with no argument at all is a marriage where one partner is consistently and unhealthily giving in. So far, so good.

But arguments are one thing, and rows are another. What makes me seriously uneasy is our new, me-generation idea that all emotions ought to be expressed all the time, and that bottling up anger is always a Bad Thing. Once you add to this the romantic idea that anger is sexy, you have an excuse for any amount of insults, plate-smashing, screaming and tears, coupled with claims that the marriage is 'a strong relationship' and 'really communicating'.

I cannot go along with this. I have seen it in action, in plenty of ill-tempered marriages, and my considered view is that as a way of life, it stinks. Expressing anger, once in a while, is pretty good fun and therapy for the angry person; and the angry person may well forget all about it and feel better afterwards. But if it is too intemperate, too uncontrolled, then the recipient of that anger will not so easily forget. Sticks and stones may break your bones, but words go right to the heart. 'My husband,' says another young wife, Maureen, 'once told me I was a selfish, stupid, fat frigid bitch. Admittedly I had just called him worse things, but the trouble is when he said that about being frigid, I couldn't forget it. Whenever we make love now, I keep thinking "that's what he thinks about me". And I sort of stop trusting him.' She is also dieting obsessively, thin though she is, because of the 'fat' bit of the insult.

An interesting American survey recently showed that women remember the detail of rows for longer than men, but men suffer too: if you shriek at your man the information that he is an insensitive bastard, an oaf, a lousy lover and a selfish swine who is obsessed with his work, you may have forgotten all about it within half an hour and be feeling much better. But he may be stricken with unhappy, quiet insecurity about his job, his sexuality and your whole relationship. Saying 'I didn't mean it' is all very well, but in that case – broods the victim – what made you say it? The old line that angry people 'always say things they don't mean' is counterbalanced by the equally old line that only when you are angry do you dare say what you really mean. And most of us have pretty total recall of things said to us in anger. They are typed, for ever, in our brains. Rows do not always clear the air: sometimes rage feeds on rage, becoming a habit or even an addiction.

And what about the children of these 'strong relationships' where anger is 'constructively expressed'? Are they in earshot? If so, believe me, they do not have a sophisticated or romantic view of what is going on. They are terrified and miserable. You are abusing them, too. They will not be there to witness the passionate reconciliation later at bedtime, will they? They will be alone in their beds, thinking frightening thoughts of divorce and loss; or creeping to one another's rooms as so many of us did in childhood, to discuss what precisely is going on and how much it threatens the home.

Couples who do row in the hearing of their children have a clear duty to explain it all afterwards, and say how sorry they were to have had a silly babyish tantrum of precisely the kind they are always telling the children not to have. But how many parents remember to do that? Secretly, worriedly, children store these things up: even in our house, where we have relatively few rows, they can remember individual ones dating back several years – even though we have carefully turned them into family jokes.

Of course there are going to be rows; the point is that they are nothing to be proud of. Not romantic, not sexy, rarely therapeutic: mainly destructive and silly and childish. One of the best pieces of marital advice I ever had was from a woman who had been married for fifty years. 'The main thing,' she said, 'is never to generalize. Never begin a sentence with "You always . . ." or "You never . . .". Be quite precise as to what you are shouting about.' It is a brilliant principle. You can say, 'You fool, you forgot to get the cleaning back, now I have nothing to wear to work, you have ruined my week!' But not 'You forgot the cleaning, you never do any simple thing for me, you are chronically selfish . . .' It is OK to say 'I am furious that I bought theatre tickets and then you forgot and worked late', but not 'You never take me out! You only care about your bloody job!' The more you generalize, the greater the damage.

Of course, if your partner does keep on committing the same crime, this may mean that you end up having an improbably huge outburst of fury over one small incident, but at least you won't have written him off entirely in your rage. You can always explain about the background to it later, calmly, in the apology-and-discussion phase.

So tread cautiously when people start advocating 'a good row to clear the air'. Count to ten, like mother told you to. Let not the sun go down upon your wrath. Don't say 'And another thing –'. Avoid irony and sarcasm at all costs. Make jokes. If all else fails, run round the block, cursing.

One thing is unequivocally comforting: the longer a marriage or partnership goes on, the better chance it has of survival. If you make it to five years the statistical probability of divorce goes down; to ten years and it goes down even further. 'By then,' said one wife, 'you know what you have got. The idea of starting afresh is appalling, throwing away all those memories . . . and hell, when you've seen a man slowly grow his pot belly and lose his front hair, and he's seen you through childbirth and tummy bugs, you're sort of committed, aren't you?'

As you decline from taffeta crinoline to baby-stained maternity dungarees, so the marriage changes too. And it goes on changing, with each new phase. The silliest thing anyone ever says is 'You're not the girl/man I married'. Of course they aren't. Neither are you. You never swim in the same river twice.

And what happened to the young Charles Darwin? Well, he made up his mind to marry, with a few pangs for lost freedom: 'Eheu! I never should know French – or see the Continent – or go to America, or go up in a Balloon, or take a solitary trip in Wales . . . never mind, my boy – cheer up – one cannot live this solitary life, with groggy old age, friendless and cold and childless, staring one in one's face . . . There is many a happy slave'.

It was a happy marriage.

4: Who's Who: Father

OK, down to the nitty-gritty. Who gets which part in the great drama of family life?

Once upon a time it was quite simple. Daddy Bear had a big chair and a big plate of porridge. Mummy Bear, a middle-sized chair and an elegantly ladylike helping of porridge. And Baby Bear knew his place. Seen and not heard.

Daddy Bear went out gathering nuts and fighting off enemies, Mummy Bear bustled round the house, Baby Bear fixed firmly to her apron-strings. There was no question of Mummy Bear wanting more porridge and taking a job in order to get it, or of Daddy Bear becoming unemployed, having a mid-life crisis and moving in with Floozie Bear, twenty years younger than him. Nor of Baby Bear turning delinquent and starting to deal in illicit substances at street corners.

Was it ever really like that? And if it was, was it happy? We could argue all day about the merits and demerits of the good old Traditional Family, but there would not be any point. The only sensible thing is to start from here. Precisely where we are. And allow for the fact that none of us is starting from quite the same place . . .

Father

Few things shake a man up more comprehensively than the news that he is to become a father. Even an eagerly planned embryo can floor him utterly. 'I had to sit down when she told me,' said one. 'Then I thought I ought to do something. Get on with it. Turn into a father. But I didn't know how.'

It is not surprising that he felt so lost. No important social image is so blurred and confused as that of the father. On the one hand, ancient notions of power and wisdom cling around the word: God the Father, Father Time, Paterfamilias. On the other hand, the prevailing cultural cliché which has grown up in this century is of 'Dad' as a lovable but rather inept stumblebum: anxious Mr Pooter, getting it wrong with his son Lupin in *Diary of a Nobody*; hen-pecked buffoons on comic postcards, working-class dads in TV sitcoms who skulk in the garden shed to escape domesticity. Father's Day cards depict the poor man exclusively in terms of carpet slippers, golf clubs, big macho dogs, fishing equipment and football scarves. A few gestures towards the 1990s are made by the inclusion of cards showing motorcycle scrambling, TV snooker-watching and windsurfing; but otherwise the run of Father's Day cards has remained virtually unchanged in thirty years. This must be terribly depressing for all those suave, sophisticated men who like to feel that they have only paused briefly in their upwardly mobile, stylish, purposeful lives in order to become the fashionably caring fathers of young children. Just because a chap did the decent thing, turned up at the birth and changed a nappy or two, it seems hard that he should be permanently stereotyped as a bluff old fogey in Prince Albert slippers, oiling his fishing rod and kicking balls. Suppose he hates all sports? Suppose what he really likes is wearing sharp suits and eating sushi, or writing sensitive experimental novels? Hard luck. Tribal mythology has cast him otherwise: the sensible, steady, conservative and deeply boring provider, to be placated with a card on Father's Day and otherwise more or less ignored . . .

Or blamed. Modern father is also bombarded by assertions from the feminist radicals that he is not necessary at all, unless for what he can donate to a handy test-tube and turkey baster; that he is, at best, tolerable. The very fact that nearly all divorces end up with the mother taking custody of the children implies that society does not believe a full-time father to be a priority. Besides, man – so the radicals tell us – is still an uncivilized, emotionally illiterate being stunted by his own forefathers' coldness. His only hope is to become a shiningly modern

New Father, present at the birth classes (not to mention the birth), bonding with his tiny baby, bathing it, changing nappies, expressing tenderness, weeping, pushing buggies, role-swapping. In the first flush of parenthood, some new men certainly do fling themselves into all this. Indeed, the divorce boom and the New Fatherhood have formed an odd alliance to produce a uniquely modern figure: the man who leaves his first wife and teenage children (having been nowhere near the birth, thank you, and never changed a nappy) then marries a much younger woman and goes enthusiastically into the birth-bath-and-potty routine. Many a balding figure now haunts Mothercare in his lunch-hour, to the secret fury of his ex-wife.

And even the New Father image fades as the children grow older: a recent sociological survey of role-reversed couples showed that half the families had reverted to a traditional pattern within two years. Once the thrill of novelty and the good resolutions wear off, if a father is out at work all day his role can very rapidly tail off into something more like the one his own father filled. Charlie Lewis, a Reading University academic who studied fatherhood in the Eighties, dispassionately observed that for all the brave talk of the New Fatherhood, 'all but a few are assistants, rather than partners, in the business of child care'.

But Lewis – in the same study – also exploded the naive modern belief that paternal tenderness was only invented by the Me generation and the feminist insistence upon paternal help. It goes deeper than that: not all past fathers have chosen the God-the-Father, remote and revered attitude. Studies of fishermen and artisans in the Victorian era revealed that rather than being brutal, drunken and aloof like the working-class father of legend, these men were very much participant, concerned members of their household, often taking the children to work alongside them. Further back, William Cobbett moved to the country in 1829 and worked at home because he believed that a child should always have a father in sight; if friends asked him to stay without his children, he did not go.

No; we did not invent paternal tenderness, but it may be

partly true that we have had, since the 1940s in Europe, to re-invent it. Two savage wars, with countless men condemned to constant, tough, adult male companionship for long stretches, have promoted machismo and dulled the conventional man's perception of his own tenderness. Nor did Freud help much: a succession of twentieth-century babycare books have deliberately marginalized the role of the father, either fearfully pointing him out as a source of future neuroses (writers before the Second World War almost universally discouraged fathers from hugging children or doing anything beyond offering a 'manly handshake'), or else joking about him, brusquely relegating him to the status of untrustworthy nurserymaid. Michael Green, in his memoirs *The Boy Who Shot Down an Airship*, puts forward the theory that it was television which undermined paternal authority. In the old days, Father was the only one in the family who had been around, gone to war perhaps, travelled the country: his memories and experiences were a child's main view of the wide world. Now that we have David Attenborough and the News bringing a far wider world into the sitting-room, who needs Dad's old war stories? It undermined paternal authority, Green says sorrowfully, to a disastrous extent. Poor old Dad. We mothers may complain of the images painted of us, but fathers have a case as well.

The good father

So what makes a good father? One feminist writer scornfully said, 'One who doesn't drink all the housekeeping, and doesn't scar the children.' If you stop people in the street they will say things like, 'Well, he should be a good provider', or 'someone for the kids to have fun with', or 'an example'. But none of these will quite do. It is dreadful to think of fathers only as financial milch-cows (because what if, through no fault of their own, they stop earning?) and it is not even vital that they should be playmates. A romping, cuddling, fun Daddy is definitely an asset, yet it is hard to ignore the fact that in cultures and classes where fathers are almost godlike in their remoteness and grandeur, plenty of perfectly well-adjusted and loving citizens manage to grow up. Successful styles of fathering vary, far more widely than styles of mothering (rather to the rage of us mothers). Look at the affection and inspiration with which John Mortimer writes about his father – an eccentric, self-willed and bruisingly ironic old barrister who would never admit that he was blind and told his son that sex was over-rated. Not an obvious social-worker's profile of perfect fatherhood, is he? But his son mourns him deeply. Or look at James Morris, whose children's love and respect survived their father's sex-change when he became Jan Morris. You can even, with a pinch of salt, embrace Nancy Mitford's comforting theory about nature's own balancing mechanism: that children of roaring, raging, whacking fathers like her own 'have enough of their father in them to enable them to weather storms in which ordinary children would lose their nerve completely'.

What is it, then, that the good father does? Some say that a father is essential to a child's moral development because 'his love tends to be conditional on performance, or good behaviour, while a mother's love is all-pervading'. (Put your writing-pads down, chaps. It is not me saying that, it is Trevor Berry, of Families Need Fathers. I toss it in only as a discussion-point.) Some say that he bolsters children's self-respect, others that he energizes the family, turns it outward to conquer the world while the mother's focus is inward, towards the hearth.

All we can be certain of is that a father is not – repeat not – a duplicate mother. When I first began writing child care books, I was challenged by the publisher as to why I kept referring to the 'mother' instead of the 'parent'. Examining my conscience, I realized that what was happening was that I was thinking of 'mother' not so much as a sex-linked word as a job description. Like accountant. Or MP, or doctor. Some fathers do indeed carry out a lot of mothering: cuddling to sleep, listening to worries about school, physical care, sorting out socks. But hovering in the back of my mind was always a certainty that fathering was a parallel – and distinctly different – function.

Later, I found that much psychological theory backs up that notion. A father is not a mother. Like it or not, he stands in a different relationship to his children: less like an extension of themselves, and more like a benevolent patron. He does different things, plays rougher games, and is less ready to identify and sympathize with every bump and worry. He laughs not only with the child, but occasionally at her. He does silly things to make her laugh, not least at herself. He is a sort of advance guard of the rough, bluff, outer world which the small child will have to meet one day: a halfway house between the utter cosy commitment of nursery life, and the world of strangers which lies beyond.

It is easy to see this in action. There are always exceptions to any stereotypes, but on the whole it is true that mothers fuss about gloves and woolly hats, whereas fathers lose them. Mothers are permanently alert for dreadful diseases in their offspring: fathers only notice when actually vomited upon. Mothers empathize, fathers sympathize. A father is often the better person to take a child along to an exam, or for a vaccination (well, so GPs tell me) because he is less likely than a mother to fall into a state of tremulous nervousness and communicate it to the child. I have seen young fathers in hospital with their children, soothing them to sleep where the mothers have failed. This does not mean that they are in any way better than the mother, but that they are different in their emotional responses.

Nature had very good reasons for arranging matters the way she did: fatherhood, as distinct from motherhood, is a necessary job. Single mothers perhaps know that better than anyone, since they have to do the fathering too, splitting themselves in half at times. However much you switch and swap, there still seem to be two roles to play in a child's life: one of them reassuring, one challenging and brave and gay. Perhaps, if there is any point at all in the concept of New Fatherhood, it is that couples feel more free to take turns at both.

So what, practically, can one say to a new father? Several things. Forgive any which are obvious. For a start, it is worth trying to get involved in the physical care of babies, but if that does not suit you or your wife, don't force it. On the one hand, as Mike Rosen the poet and often full-time father observes, 'Being involved with all the poo and sick and stuff actually makes the relationship better and cuddlier. Also all the singing to sleep.' On the other hand, I know a kind, beloved, humorous, much-cherished and conscientious father who only ever changed a nappy once. He was sick. His wife then had to clean up two messes instead of one, and never asked him again. Horses for courses, I say.

The second thing to say is, Be Around. There is a dreadful tendency for men (and some high-powered working women) to think that unless they are doing formal quality-time things with their children, or 'minding' them with no other adult in sight, there is no advantage whatever in being present, and you might as well be at work, or out. This is not so. Rosen once wrote a lovely account of the kind of domestic pottering, the background presence, which children need from both parents at times. His theory, in his wonderfully blokey book *Goodies and Daddies*

(every new Dad should have one), is that wiping the table, doing the school run, tidying the mantelpiece is time you use to make a relationship with your children. 'It's then that they ask the really important things – Do buffaloes eat spaghetti? – and other vital questions. Even reading the paper, your presence is a great big affirmation that you like the company you're keeping, just as your absence creates the tiny anxiety that home isn't where you want to be and the children aren't who you want to be with. If you are around, the children will claim you.'

And this is probably one of the hardest lessons for fathers to learn. Some learn it a very hard way indeed: Sir John Harvey-Jones, the industrialist, in his memoirs laid out mercilessly how he nearly let professional ambition sabotage his life. Rising through the ranks at ICI in the Sixties, he starkly describes how corrupting that world was to his family life. 'I started to behave politically – not dishonourably, I hope, but deliberately seeking to demonstrate that I was better than others. I played at tycoons, threw myself into jet-set life, drinking and nightclubbing. I neglected my wife and daughter and took them for granted. In that brief period I messed up my family life badly.' He spotted it in time, and renewed it. But his description must have struck a chord with many men: caught in the dilemma of wanting to be a good provider – a top provider – and a good father.

Business and industry are only very slowly accepting that fathers need to 'be around' for their children; one headhunter brutally observed that if a man mentioned at interview that on some days he might need to be off sharp at five to get his child from nursery school, 'it would be the kiss of death'. Another man I knew, a salesman working from home, regularly spent time caring for his three children while his wife ran her own small business. 'I work out my time flexibly, and do the paperwork late at night,' he said. 'But they would be livid if they found out.' In some firms, men can successfully move into a slower lane for a while in early fatherhood, as many women do. Britain reeled with shock in the late Eighties when a cabinet minister, Norman Fowler, gave up his post in order to spend more time with his young children, saying, 'I have not been the best of sharing fathers, and I want to be home more for a while.' He was back three years later, when his girls were older. There was a good deal of media sniggering about the whole manoeuvre (at one point nobody but me, in all the British press, seemed to believe in his motives), but when I polled a carriageful of rail commuters on the matter, they were unanimous.

'Lucky blighter,' said one young man. 'Good for him. I wish I could do it. I never see my kids awake except at the weekend, and I travel two weekends in three.' 'My wife,' said another, 'had to make the decision about which nursery school my son goes to. I wanted to go and see it myself, but I couldn't get the day off.' None of the men wanted to drop out, or reverse roles; they just wanted space to experience family life in the irreplaceable early years, and, as another said, 'to lay a foundation of good memories against the time he becomes a horrible teenager who despises his old Dad'. Another, interestingly, observed that since he had lost a high-powered job and taken a less good one, the time he spent with his children was better and more relaxed. 'I used to be so hyped up that I had to spend my free time blowing off violent energy, driving to the coast at 90 m.p.h. to go ocean-racing, or playing ferocious squash. I couldn't wind down, ever. Now I'm a bit of a vegetable at work, I have a more balanced kind of time with the kids. I like it, actually.'

Men who slow down their careers on purpose, though, are exceptional and brave. Society still applauds the macho workaholic, and high-pressure jobs make you feel important. Children, whatever their other merits, rarely do. Any mother can tell you about that gloomy, isolated moment when the joys of family life are reduced to a kitchenful of spilt cat-litter and a cross, snotty toddler. In the words of another writer, Fraser Harrison, at a certain period of his family life 'Their little ways ceased to be charming and eccentric, becoming instead infuriatingly self-centred. Their incessant noise was no longer a merry chorus to our household life, but a clamorous and grating din.' At such times a company chauffeur at the door and a sheaf of policy decisions seem like blessed freedom.

Balance is the key. And courtesy, and respect. Perhaps we

should be nicer to fathers, celebrate them more. I know it seems hard, when mothers feel so chronically unappreciated; but a bit of mutual respect can work wonders.

Even if it does not get the lost gloves, and woolly hats, and bits of school uniform found.

Fathers and sons

Scratch the surface of the newest New Man and you find a hunter who wants his boy to go out hunting with him. A mild, sensitive chap considerably startled me recently by looking at his boy-and-girl twins and saying sadly of the girl, 'She's everything one would want in a son – athletic, bold, tall, strong . . . and look at him.' The little boy cowered sweetly behind his mother, inches smaller and far more nervous than his bouncing minx of a sister.

Men have to keep a tight rein on their expectations of their sons, because sons constantly measure themselves against their fathers, and it would be a terrible strain to have both of them playing the same game. Boys easily start to feel that they have disappointed their fathers, and this makes them sad and surly. Think American-therapist-speak: the correct message for a father to project is, 'Gee, son, I am proud of you. Whatever you do.' If the son in question is actually lying on the sofa with the curtains shut at four o'clock in the afternoon, a Walkman clamped to his ears, trying to turn on the television with a horrible gnarled yellow toe protruding from a hole in his sock, this is difficult. The message may then be mutated to, 'Gee, son, I just know you've got unique gifts you could be using, is there any way I can help you to use them?' He will grunt, but it will be a pleased sort of grunt.

Re-reading the above, it sounds a bit soft-headed to me, too. Blame the fact that I have just come back from a Sports Day where the father of an eleven-year-old who came second – second – in a major race was heard shouting at him for not being first. Think about it.

Fathers and Daughters

I worked with a man once whom I rather disliked, most of the time: a snappy, shallow, style junkie, he was. But his Achilles heel was his daughter, about whom he would rave incessantly. 'From the first moment she was born . . . oh God, the first little pair of red shoes . . . she's gorgeous, I tell you, gorgeous . . . marvellous girl, I could eat her . . .' When I saw her it was quite a shock: she was twelve, extremely lumpen, dough-faced, lank-haired and shy. The kind of female this fashionable man would normally never be seen in the same room with. But he folded her in his arms and pushed her forwards saying 'Isn't she gorgeous?' without a trace of irony, and she smiled happily. I really loved that annoying man, at that moment.

In order to grow up confident, daughters truly do need their fathers' approbation. This applies to physical, as well as moral, good points. It is absolutely not a father's role to point out his daughter's spots, peculiar dress sense, or rolls of puppy-fat. Mothers can do this more tactfully, and cousins and aunts more tactfully still. A father's job is to be his daughter's first devoted and chivalrous admirer. However, when her first boyfriends appear on the scene, his role is not to grill the poor spotty youths on their employment prospects and honourable intentions. It is to retire to the potting shed and have a good weep.

One other thing. Some men are so appalled by stories of child abuse that they are afraid to hug their children, especially daughters. I know a man, call him Mick, who adores his five-year-old daughter from her gold hair to her red shoes. But ever since another little girl on his street was almost raped by a drunken stepfather, in a case which shook the neighbourhood, Mick won't take her on his knee. 'It's better for her, in these wicked times,' he says. He is confused and upset; Emma cannot understand why her father now jumps out of bed when she creeps in every morning. Time may bring them a compromise, but for the moment the situation is desperately sad. As it is in society at large: fathers may still take their daughters swimming, but more and more of them are refusing to take their daughters' friends. Revolting and baffling though paedophilia is to most of us, cases of it send echoes of unhappiness through ordinary families.

It must not be the end of paternal tenderness. Every parent knows that children are cuddly, a physical delight. Soft cheeks against your own, heads burrowing in your shoulder, games of rubbing noses and a happy nonsense vocabulary of snuzzles and pouncies and eaty-all-uppies are part of a happy family life, sometimes until the children are quite enormous. A baby who is not hugged will pine or even die. Older children, suddenly finding hugs withdrawn, will feel odd and lonely. You have to hug, when it is welcome.

And when it is not welcome you have to refrain from hugging. The lesson of privacy and dignity is important too: parents – but especially Daddies, who represent strength and mastery to a child – must not pounce and hug too much when the child resists it, or is busy trying to do something else. And no child ever should have to kiss anyone, however related to them, unless they feel like it. But you can always plead for a hug, if you're desperate . . .

5: Who's Who: Mother

A Little Fable

Mother 1994 fell asleep, the night before Mother's Day, having supped unwisely on chocolate mousse and the children's unfinished Marmite sandwiches. On such nights, warning nightmares swirl around the sleeper, with ghosts appearing in threes like Ebenezer Scrooge's tormentors. And so it was. The first apparition loomed at the foot of the bed, with chains of bread-dough fettering its wrinkled hands. It was a stoutish, greying figure with a fixed smile. Its hair was parted in the middle, a white apron pinned upon its broad bosom, and around it clung a homely smell of cakes and ironing.

'I,' it said chattily, 'am the ghost of Motherhood Past. That's my picture, on the Mother's Day cards.'

'What did you do?' asked the dreamer.

The ghost bridled. 'Do? I baked. I made all my own jam and pickles. I rose in the dawn to cook proper hot breakfasts. I sang as I scrubbed the front step. I sewed little shirts for my babies, taught them their letters and never failed to read a Bible story aloud each evening. For twelve years I was always there at the school gate, and when my treasures left home –' she sniffed, 'I gave them stamps to post their laundry home. I was the heart of the family.' She paused, and sniffed.

The dreamer waited, then timidly asked, 'Um, what happened to you in the end?'

The ghost sniffed again, louder. 'When the children grew up my husband ran off with a bimbo,' it said morosely. 'He said I had no conversation. And I was forty-five and I couldn't get a job because they said I had no skills. Bah!'

It vanished abruptly, leaving only a faint smell of scorching linen in the air. A second ghost appeared, fidgeting nervously as it spoke. The thing wore a neat business suit and laddered tights, at which it plucked distressfully. It carried a briefcase, a season ticket and three plastic carrier bags out of which protruded rolls of toilet paper, a length of track for a model railway, a cabbage, a packet of spaghetti and a paperback on Stress. Glancing at its watch, it spoke rapidly.

'I am the ghost of Motherhood Present, OK? I took maternity leave twice, always got back after twelve weeks. I've found a wonderful nursery, honestly; the only thing is it likes the children out at five-thirty sharp, and the school comes out even sooner, so Damien has to have a key, and I have to dash like mad if the departmental meeting overruns. And I do believe in Quality Time with children, don't you? So we're reading *The Lion the Witch and the Wardrobe* and making cardboard sundials and learning Italian together in the evenings, and of course on Thursdays it's Suzuki violin, but the trouble is if I have to stay late at the office we miss the beginning of the class and the teacher gets cross with me, in Japanese, especially if I haven't practised enough with him, and on Saturdays I do the week's cooking for the freezer, because I do believe in home-made food, don't you? – only there's the office paperwork, and I have to do a lot of the washing by hand because the machine goes funny and plumbers won't come at weekends . . . but I've bought this new Time Manager personal computer, it's all a matter of efficiency –'

The dreamer interrupted. 'What happened to you in the end?'

'Well, I'm still at work,' twitched the ghost. 'My son Damien became a Buddhist monk, said he liked the quiet, and Jocasta lives in a squat and writes poetry, and says my lifestyle is really gross and materialistic. But they always got their Quality Time. And I've kept my full pension entitlement.'

Mother 1993, half waking from the nightmare, thought dimly to herself that nothing could be worse. But in an unearthly glare, a new and dreadful figure was stumping towards her. Indescribable, it was – whether human or robot she could hardly tell, with its mass of wires and arms and doors, knobs and levers and loudspeakers and shrink-wrapped Mini Kiev dispensers. But from its centre came a human voice.

'I am the ghost of Motherhood Yet to Come,' it said resolutely. 'I rejected the mistakes of the past. I refused to be a cosy domestic slave, nor yet a workaholic, guilt-ridden wreck. In 1991 the European Community directed me to go back to the workplace where my skills were needed. And the magazine writers told me not to be guilty about delegating. So I delegated.'

'What?' asked the dreamer, fascinated.

'Everything!' replied the ghost proudly. 'I even managed to write a whole annual report during my last labour, because I had an epidural Caesarean done privately, rather than waste my precious time pushing. Now I bleep Nanny and a cleaner and an au pair for nights, and we buy microwave food, and there's a marvellous mail-order toyshop which chooses all the presents according to psychological profiles, and wraps them in time for the birthdays. Last year they both got Walkmans and story tapes, so that takes care of bedtime. As a treat they are allowed to Dial-a-Parent and these marvellous professionals, therapists and things, talk over their problems.'

'Do they like all this delegating?' asked the dreamer.

'Naturally,' said the echoing voice in the creature's empty centre. 'Any problems with their behaviour, the school generally sends me a fax to let me know that the computer has booked them in with the educational psychologist, and a bleep Nanny to programme their favourite supper into the microwave and have a nice video biked round.' Suddenly, the voice grew distorted. 'Hang on – there's a problem – the Nanny's broken down – malfunction alert – the bleeper isn't coding in – System Failure, System Failure, Malfunction alert –' Somewhere, a child cried.

Mother 1993 was quite happy to wake up to the usual sight of piles of ironing, wonky school-made cards, cold toast and stewed tea on a loving tray with a daffodil, and the feeling of warm little bodies creeping into the bed. She resolved to give up all attempts at perfection, overachievement and time-and-motion efficiency, and put up with life more or less as it was. As we all do.

Real mothers

Since everything one writes about children and family life is also about mothers, it seems superfluous to consider them separately. But there are one or two observations about the mother in the family which are worth making. Even if nobody seems to believe any longer that Mother Knows Best. Even if Germaine Greer (sweet supportive thing!) once described a conventional mother as 'the dead heart of the family, spending father's earnings on consumer goods'. Even if nobody seems to understand us . . .

The first thing which must be admitted is that motherhood is a powerful mind-altering drug. You only have to talk to people who have overdosed on it (say, by having ten children) to discover how high it is possible to get. Motherhood makes you bossy and self-assured, yet unconfident in your role in the outside world (ask poor women returners-to-work with grown-up children who let themselves be patronized by short-skirted bimbos twenty years younger and a lot dimmer). Motherhood makes you as fierce and bold as a tigress defending her young (say, in a lackadaisical hospital casualty department), and yet racked with guilt that you are not doing better. It makes you secure in your children's unconditional love, and yet quiveringly vulnerable to every passing worry about them. Motherhood can make you, for a while, unrecognizable to your oldest friends. The single, childless ones may actually shun you for a few years, so odd have you become.

Relax. All this is quite natural. You get over it. You will never be quite the same again, true; but everyone grows up, and it just happens that motherhood has turned out to be part of your personal growing process. The effects of the drug weaken as children grow older; by the time the baby is three, you can sometimes think about other things; by the time it is at school you might start fancying a career again (even if you have been doing one all the time, you may well have been on autopilot. I certainly was). Who knows, by the time your youngest child is eight or nine, you might even feel like some late nights out dancing. And when your children reach their teens, it is more than possible that you will be looking around wildly for more interesting work, old friends, and adventure of every kind. The trick, at that point, is finding where they have all disappeared to.

For if the problem for fathers lies in realizing that they are fathers, and getting down to being fathers, the problem for mothers is the opposite: preventing yourself from getting lost in the role. If you do lose your own identity, the risk is that you start trying to find it through the children, projecting your own ambitions on to them. 'Samantha so loves her music, of course I was going to be a professional violinist myself, but she's really so dedicated . . .' trills a mother whose daughter, it is plain to any onlooker, only moderately enjoys playing the violin and has no intention of making it a life-work. Or even worse, you might start making a career out of improving your children with arcane accomplishments and certificates, to make them better than the substandard children next door. 'We really feel that the school fees and the tennis coaching and dancing tuition have been an investment.' No harm spending the money, or organizing the music-lessons, of course; the harm comes in colonizing your children's individuality and trying to shape them to your own ends because deep down you feel that you gave up your own individuality and ambitions by having them, so it serves them right.

Bossing

Another worrying effect of motherhood as a mind-bending drug is the way it can lead you to start inflicting the fiercest kind of mothering on other people who don't need it, or want it. Like husbands. While a few men like being bossed around by women and told to put their warm vests on or go on a diet, many do not like it one little bit. Sometimes they absent-mindedly put up with it, because in the general maelstrom of family life this mother-person seems to be issuing orders to everyone in the same tone: 'Ronnie, get your cub uniform ready! Janey, help him with the drawer if it's stuck! Marie-Christine, have you got the baby dressed? Down, Bonzo! Get your mucky paws off the sofa! Someone put the cat out! Darling, tuck your shirt in, and you can't wear that shirt with that tie.' Sometimes, after many years of this, men surprise everybody by slinking off with a much younger woman, like their secretary, and everybody assumes that it's all about sex. It could, however, partly be because after being snapped at like a recalcitrant labrador or two-year-old for too long, with none of the corresponding advantages of being able to lie around all day panting, or getting birthday parties with candles, the poor man just enjoyed having someone look up to him and take orders off him, instead. No, no, it's no excuse. Just a thought.

So crack the whip by all means, keep the show on the road; but in being a mother, do not lose the art of being a good companion, a grown-up, fun to be with and with a mind of your own capable of soaring above the circus-ring of family life. Stage a token walk-out occasionally: to the cinema, for a weekend away with a girlfriend, or to see a play that only you are interested in. When I became badly stressed and ratty one winter, I quite coincidentally started getting into a routine which meant that, instead of one night per week away from home and the rest at my desk here, I had to spend two nights away, one of them staying with a woman friend in her quiet, tidy, child-free London house. After ten years of assuming that if I vanished for more than twenty-four hours family life would collapse entirely in ruins, I was nervous and tearful about this and assumed that it would be an extra strain. But – surprise! I found I adored my extra night, slacker routine, less frantic travelling; and the different company, the odd party even, and the quiet, adult start to the next day. And of course the family were fine under the command of the deputy-ringmaster, their father, or occasionally of a babysitter. They did become addicted to some seriously trashy Monday night television programmes, but that was a small price to pay for the resident wife and mother coming home relaxed, beaming and glad to be around.

I also came back with a different angle on their problems: more able to get a reasonable perspective on a school difficulty, for instance, or someone's row with a friend, or my husband's professional dilemmas. Everybody benefited, in the same way as they benefit when I have been reading something stimulating, or surprising, or challenging in a new field. Stressed, overworked modern mothers – possibly with an outside job – tend to feel dreadfully guilty about reading, say, *A Brief History of Time,* or watching a documentary about Chinese medicine, or wandering around the house with a particularly gripping novel, but the odds are that the input from these things will contribute rapidly, and directly, to the way they talk to their families and the wisdom they bring to managing them. The more we see of the world outside, the more confident we are in roles other than that of mother, the more certain we will feel of our own ground, our own judgement, our own vision. The mothers who fall for every foible and fashion of child care are the mothers who are too utterly immersed in it, to the exclusion of the rest of life. Look up, look around, and be sceptical.

Smother love

Don't do it. Fathers need telling this, too. It is really about children, but I deliberately raise it under the heading of Mothers because mothers do it most. All right, not to mince matters, we are famous for it. Overprotection of children, even rather large tough children, is a modern epidemic. For one thing, mass communication makes us daily more neurotically aware of the vile things that happen – most often at the extremes of society – to children who are not protected enough. Less laudably, I suspect that we have become extra-passionately protective of our own children simply because we don't have as many as we used to: birth control has reduced the average family to just over two, with an ever-growing number of only children. Who remembers that old expression 'As fussy as a hen with one chick'? There you are.

Furthermore, irrespective of the actual risk on the streets, society has seen a steadily growing *belief* in street violence and public lawlessness, which has unfortunately coincided with the rise of television and video. The result is that huge numbers of us have frankly lost the habit of going out much: the last survey of British habits showed that over eighty percent of the population's idea of a recreational evening was not to visit the cinema or the town centre or a football match, but to stay in with a curry and a video. Our children, on the other hand, do want to go out. So we choke on our curry and listen for the telephone while they roam at large in the terrible Outside World. Every time a dreadful thing befalls a child or teenager, we scan the news for some comforting evidence that he was out at a time, or in a place, where ours would not have been. If we don't find it, we tighten the house rules further.

Yet, when they are eighteen, our children will get an inalienable legal right to set out on their own into a world full of fast-running rivers, heavy traffic, drug dealers, deviants, muggers, rapists and misleading signposts. They will probably live alone, and will not always have the money for a taxi fare home.

However much it hurts, our duty to protect them is diluted by an equal duty to prepare them for the real world. Telling them about it is not enough: they have to get in the midst of it and dodge the missiles themselves. To provide a safe bolt-hole for them is not only the least we can do; perhaps it is also the most any of us should do.

But when are you overprotecting, and when merely being a responsible parent? How long is a piece of string? Take new babies. In the eighteenth century the followers of philosophers Locke and Rousseau preached the doctrine of 'hardening' children in the Spartan style, rather like hardening off pot plants, by laying them on planks to sleep, underdressing them in cold weather and plunging them in icy baths. In the 1920s a popular babycare guru in the US called John B. Watson advised parents to put the baby out in a fenced yard and to 'Be sure to dig some holes in the yard so it has to crawl in and out of them. Let it learn to overcome difficulties almost from the moment of birth, away from your watchful eye'. You could, he conceded, install a periscope to watch the baby if you absolutely had to.

Both authorities were mildly nutty, to be sure (most of us child care writers are. Never believe all of what anyone says in books like this). But have you ever watched a mother with her first adored child, officiously helping it over every small obstacle, never letting it discover the limits of its own stretching or lifting power? Have you never itched to pull her hands off the levers of power for a few minutes, and let little Johnny discover personally that if he gets on the pushalong bus the wrong way round, he won't find the steering-wheel?

Our hands shoot out to stop babies toppling, toddlers falling in the fire – but they often shoot out too readily, merely to prevent smaller frustrations, knocks and setbacks. I remember once in fascinated horror watching a surgeon allow his child to play with a door-hinge: but he had, he said, calculated exactly how much damage the child could cause with the hinge that way round, and that it wasn't severe; he had warned the child repeatedly, and now it was time to allow a minor accident. I am not sure I could be that chilly about it, but he had a point.

When the child grows up a little, a new stage comes. He can pour out his own apple-juice into the mug, but he spills a bit. Next time he might not spill it, because he has worked out how it happened; but the question is whether there will be a next time, because you might fussily take over again, having 'proved' he can't be trusted. He goes to playgroup: a big girl pushes him. Do you have the nerve to wait and see if he pushes back? Or do you sweep down and sort out the quarrel before it has a chance to develop any further?

Time goes on: at school, there is a test. Your daughter does badly, and your instinct is to protect her from knowing, or at least from caring. But her best friend then goes off with another girl to make snide remarks in a corner, and suddenly – panickingly – you realize that you can't protect her. More and more perils crowd in: there are no seat belts on the school bus, the maths teacher has a bitter and sarcastic tongue, the big boys call the little ones rude names in the playground. None of the perils is quite big enough to tackle forthrightly, but it still hurts to watch fate's assaults upon your child, your treasured one who has never ridden a bike without a crash-helmet, never walked home alone or missed a dental check-up. Grimly, you realize the narrow limits of what you can actually do.

Teenage years loom. You see ever more clearly that although you long to be a strong protecting wall, the only way to do it is to become a jailer. It may be painfully obvious to you that the boy or girl your baby has brought home is a nasty, flashy cruel piece of work, but dare you say it? You know the kind of unpleasant men who accost fourteen-year-old girls in cinemas, but are you really going to insist on chaperoning three competent teenagers through some Kevin Costnerama when they know you're bored stiff by it? All your sons' friends catch the bus on their own to the football ground on Saturday: are you really going to drive him there in the Volvo and see him safely in? To weigh a theoretical danger against an overwhelming love is the hardest thing in the world.

Or perhaps the hardest thing is to give up your own judgement in favour of someone else's. Suppose your child wants to go on an Adventure Survival course, and he's never lasted more than a three-mile family stroll without getting blisters; how are you going to protect him? Not, I hope, in the way one family of my acquaintance once did: they bribed their fourteen-year-old to give up the idea of a youth club hiking holiday by giving him a video recorder of his own. They thought the walking would be too much for him (his youth leader disagreed) and that he wouldn't manage to keep his own kit dry and organized (his youth leader disagreed, again). Such parents are of the sad type who seem to pop up at their children's drug trials later saying 'We gave him the best of everything!' in an aggrieved tone of voice, as if shelling out for a personal TV and a private-school education ought to provide insurance against human frailty for ever.

Mothers – and a few fathers – will always want to protect their children a little too much; the saving, balancing factor is that the children themselves resist it so fiercely. The trouble – no, the glory – is that our children are not blasé. They want to do new things, risk failure, meet different people who don't share the family consensus. It isn't just the quest for the opposite sex; my best times as a teenager were chatting to strangers on buses, doing the ironing down at the local Cyrenian shelter for down-and-outs, and being lectured on life by the tramps and dossers; or trying to get some sense out of the spaced-out cult smiles down at the Hare Krishna temple. My brothers all took up parachuting, brushing off all objections from their tremulous elders with the words 'Look, we want us to survive too, you know'. My parents no doubt didn't like any of these activities, and I shall be a bag of nerves when my own children start exposing themselves to the outside world. I pray for strength and cool judgement then. Perhaps I will hold in my mind, as a talisman, the memory of a millionaire's daughter I once met: her father's bodyguard drives her to and from school and the only recreation she is allowed in the outer world is being driven to horse shows with her prize ponies, accompanied by grooms and her mother. From fortune-hunters, kidnappers, rapists and other perils of the modern world this child is indeed safe: safe as in a harem, safe as a bird in a gilded cage.

Another child I shall think of is a slightly mentally handicapped boy, brought up by his parents with close protective care, allowed to do odd menial jobs for pocket money but waited on and pitied and protected at every turn. He became seventeen; the old couple died. Those of us who knew the boy were terrified of what might happen. But he bore himself with dignity through the funerals, and was soon living in a sheltered flat and holding down a regular handyman job. The pity of it is that his parents would have been so proud to see it; but while they were there, it couldn't have happened. We must warn, we must prepare, we must protect; but we must let go.

A man I knew, a silversmith, made his daughter a simple pendant for her fifteenth birthday. Inside it he put three tightly rolled and folded fifty-pound notes, representing a taxi fare home from almost anywhere. He arranged the pendant so that it could be unscrewed to release the emergency money – but only once, after which he would need to repair it. That way, he reasoned, she couldn't spend the money on clothes or shoes as a silly impulse, but would always be able to get home at any hour, or book into a hotel alone if the company she fell into seemed threatening. He is dead now, and his daughter is nearly forty. But she still wears the pendant: it symbolizes at once her freedom and her father's protection.

Mothers and Sons

A boy's best friend is his mother. Um, perhaps. But it does not hurt to brood a little on the darker side of all this – if only to get a line on whatever is going on between one's mother-in-law and one's husband. And what may start going on, as he grows up, between you and that dear little moppet of a boy who used to nestle so confidingly (sob!) on your shoulder and nuzzle your bosom with such flattering appreciation.

Write this down somewhere, in letters of fire, and contemplate it occasionally: boys have to get away from their mothers. They come back, of course. But they seem to have to cross that river, to prove that they are male, to leave the womenfolk behind. And it makes them quite frightfully rude and ungrateful, for a spell. Some of them never change: Bernard Shaw said, 'Of all human struggles, there is none so treacherous and remorseless as that between the artist man and the mother woman'; other writers, such as John Osborne, Dennis Potter and Colin McInnes, have written about mothers – even if not necessarily their own – in terms so intemperate that one gasps. Somerset Maugham said that 'few misfortunes can befall a boy which bring worse consequences than to have a really affectionate mother', and D.H. Lawrence, melodramatic old number that he was, lamented that 'Nobody can have the soul of me. My mother had it, and nobody can come into my very self again'. A whole boarding-school culture grew up among the British upper-classes to ensure the early divorce of a boy from the dreadful, unwholesome, cloying, retarding company of Mummy.

In ordinary family life, therefore, the nicest boys turn strangely surly towards their mothers at certain points. 'Look, Mum, I'm ten,' they say, 'I can look after myself.' Mummies daft enough to continue invading the bathroom and peering in ears once their sons object to it are riding for a bad fall. And yet boys need their mothers' affection desperately, even while they reject it. The only way round it which seems to work is humour, from early on: ham it up, pose as a daft-old-Mummy, allow them their feelings of power and supremacy. We have long had a running fantasy joke, my son and I, about how he becomes an astronaut, chairman of ICI, Prime Minister or whatever, and I burst into his spaceship or cabinet room in worried Jewish-Momma style, quavering 'My boy! Are you wearing your warm vest! I brought you a hot-water bottle for your poor kidneys!' The extreme absurdity of this has seemed – ever since maleness first surfaced in earnest at about seven – to cheer him up. If I can see that it wouldn't do to burst in on a Prime Minister, he figures to himself, perhaps I will show some tact about kissing him in front of his schoolfriends.

Although, of course, when the boy requires you to mutate back into a protective, all-wise Rock of Ages – do so.

Mothers and Daughters

The trouble with girl babies, a group of us once guiltily agreed, is that you find yourself being harder on them from the start. A boy is a strange alien miracle, sprung from your body. A girl is yourself, over again. Therefore, being hard on yourself, you expect more of the girl. It is observable that toddler girls (unless they have over-doting Daddies, q.v.) tend to fuss, cry, and create less than their allegedly macho, tough, masculine brothers. Probably because their mothers don't put up with it.

Girls also tend to help more around the house than boys. Yes, yes, I know: it is reprehensible typecasting. It worries me no

end. But I begin to see how it happens: the cruel fact is that in the pre-teen years at least, it is just less trouble to get girls to clear the table and run errands than to make boys do it. Exhausted mothers with a child of each sex have a choice between asking once, and asking fifteen times with threats: they often take the line of least resistance. In our house when this happens everyone is trained to raise the cry 'No Islamic Practices!' – which may be a bit of a caricature of Islam, but makes the point succinctly.

As little girls grow up, it is every day more vital for their mothers to give them plenty of space to grow. Despite those treacherous feelings of identification, your daughter is not you, young again. You may have been a beauty and a coquette, but it is her right to turn out to be a solid, serious, aspiring veterinary surgeon with thick legs. You may have been academically brilliant and the Head Girl, she may be a minxy little party girl or a mumsy thing who longs to become a nursery nurse. Leave her be. Enjoy her differences from you. And do not be jealous of her. It is perfectly true that the new generation have a lot more fun and far more options than we did. That is our achievement, as a generation of women. It is not something to get resentful about, however ungrateful the little beasts seem to be.

6: Who's Who: Children

All the worst excesses of parenthood, throughout history, have come from the fatal tendency of adults to think of children as being property rather than people. Granted, this has resulted in them being carefully guarded; it has also resulted in extreme cruelty, because all power tends to corrupt. We may smile, or groan, at some of the wider effects of modern legislation on children – like the warning given by a leading British teachers' union recently that if a teacher shouted at a difficult child in class he or she could be sued by that child for 'emotional abuse' – but anything is better than a situation where adults may, at their whim and that of their society, impose almost any cruelty on their offspring.

If you want salutary proof that the sane, common-sense maternal instinct is a fragile plant, look at the evidence of history. Mothers have always been all too easily persuaded by society to do dreadful things, honestly believing there was a good reason. From the Middle Ages onwards they beat small children violently because so many died young – the more repressive sorts of Christianity filled them with a fear that unless sin was beaten out of them, the children would go to hell. One eighteenth-century mother wrote plaintively, 'I have got a pain in my back with whipping Susan today, who struggled so that I have got a wrench.' They swaddled babies tightly to stop their limbs growing crooked, not knowing that it was rickets which caused the crookedness and that the swaddling itself almost guaranteed dislocated hips. John Evelyn, the seventeenth-century diarist, told how his niece was crushed to death at two years old by a restraining garment, an iron bodice. Because crawling was considered by Victorian mothers to be 'bestial' and undignified, early baby-walker devices tormented infants into the upright position whether they liked it or not; if children masturbated their fingers would be fastened behind their backs with finger-stocks, if they slouched a backboard was lashed to their spines. Collectors of such things can show you poisonous laxatives, lethal opiates like 'Mother Bailey's Quieting Syrup', and terrifying books like *Joyful Deaths of Young Children*.

One such collector, Sally Kevill-Davies, a rector's wife from Hertfordshire, showed me her assembly of such terrible things once and drew a conclusion I have never forgotten. 'I do not believe there is a maternal instinct,' she said sadly. 'One of the most ironic and depressing facts about child care is the way in which ignorance, superstition and imperfectly applied reasoning appear to have triumphed over instinct and sense.'

Even today, with reason, we obey science and received wisdom over instinct (well, how else could you bring yourself to hand over a healthy baby for a vaccination that will make it, however briefly, unwell?) How can we be haughty about the medical horrors of past ages (opium grains put under babies' fingernails as a soother, solid food forced into newborn mouths to cure diarrhoea) when it is not so long since parents insisted that doctors remove adenoids and tonsils as a routine (and sometimes appendices before they sent the child to boarding-school, as a precaution against having their holidays disrupted)? How can we be smug about laudanum syrups of the nineteenth century, when question-marks still hang over such things as the chemicals used in cot-mattresses? We may laugh, now, at such social foibles as the way earlier generations used wet-nurses, or banned bananas because they might overstimulate sexual appetite, or placed little girls' noses in an iron press to correct their shape; but what will future generations make of such modern eccentricities as 'hothousing' newborn babies with constant stimulation, or 'in-womb education' through tapes? Of the British fetish for early boarding school, or the American one for teeth-braces worn throughout adolescence in the quest for the perfect, dazzling, all-white smile? Cruelties have always been practised on children in the name of sanctity or science or social graces, and probably always will be.

So the governance of children should probably be reduced to the bare minimum. Minimalist parenting could well be the coming thing. Not quite, perhaps, to the extent that Rousseau advocated, of letting them survive in a wild state and never teaching table-manners; but certainly we could do with a step back from the degree of interference which has become fashionable in recent years. It sometimes seems, from the media, that half the Western world is living in a depressed underclass which lets its children roam the streets unchecked, ram-raiding and mugging old ladies; while the other half drives them frantically around in cars from educational psychologist to violin-lesson, pausing only to buy more videos and computer games lest the offspring become bored.

Which is, of course, rubbish. I see, in all kinds of homes, a remarkable amount of pragmatic good sense being applied to parenting. And a lot of minimalism, too. Especially since the recession meant everyone – especially the gullible middle-classes – having less money to spend on nonsense. It has concentrated our minds wonderfully on the essentials. Children have to be fed, clothed against the elements, conversed with a great deal, protected from evildoers and poisons, and given the chance to play and read and observe the adult world. They have to be educated, to take in the knowledge and wisdom their society has developed, and encouraged to take it further as they grow up. They have to be loved and valued, and allowed to bestow their own love on family and friends. And that is enough for anyone to take on, without any better-baby routines, hot-housing, social drilling, fussy dressing or general competitive nastiness. Children are not feathers in their parents' hats. Most parents know this perfectly well.

But neither are they miniature adults, with precisely the same rights and freedoms as adults. They have different rights, like the ones I have just mentioned; and there are some areas where their rights are as limited as their abilities. A baby does not have the right to crawl unhampered into the fire; and a teenage girl does not have the right to stay out all night hitch-hiking along the bypass in a tight leather skirt. Sometimes parents forget to be parents, for one of several reasons. Maybe they want to be the child's 'best friend' instead: this happens at times with kind and devoted single parents, lonely for other adult company, who with the best of intentions give at once too much responsibility and too much freedom to their child (it is usually a lone child who gets this treatment). Sometimes parents won't be parents because they have never quite stopped being children themselves (who has not seen a father sulking because his son won't play with him? Or a mother jealous of her daughter's carefree nights out at silly teenage parties?)

What do they want?

I conducted, two years ago, an interview with my own six- and eight-year-olds on what exactly they expected of family life. It was quite revealing:

Me: What do you think mothers and fathers are for?

8-year-old: Looking after children. And training them.

Me: Well, I don't like the word training. You can't train people like you train dogs, can you? You can try, but they only end up shouting a lot. You have to keep children safe and give them things to do and think about, and show them how to be nice . . .

6-year-old: And feed them properly. It's teatime.

Me: No it isn't. Anyway –

6-year-old: And you have to stop them doing too much bum talk. And naughty poems. I think naughty poems are very bad. There's one VERY BAD one, it goes 'Old King Cole was a merry old soul . . .'

Me (interrupting hastily): Yes, yes. Some parents get far too worried about smutty talk –

6-year-old (continuing regardless): '. . . The WC was engaged, and so was the kitchen sink –' (*finishes rhyme, unfit for respectable publisher to print*). Anyway, that's a very bad one. I don't think it should be allowed. I know an even worse one –

8-year-old: Parents ought to stop brothers and sisters fighting. It's a Mummy's job to calm them down.

Me: How, exactly?

8-year-old: I don't know. Shout at them, I suppose. Do you ever worry about bossing people too much in your books and your family?

Me: Yes, all the time. But mothers tend to get bossy.

6-year-old: So do school dinner ladies. They're far too strict with children at playtime. There ought to be a law against it.

8-year-old: I don't think it's fair for parents to read books so they can sneakily improve their child, like a cactus in a pot. If children want to be violent and watch videos all day, it's half their choice. If they want to grow up sensible and dignified, they can. Children have their own choice about being perfect and nice or not, haven't they?

6-year-old: But they really ought to be fed properly. And on time.

So I did. But my son, eight at the time, had hit on the nub of the matter. How children grow up is, indeed, half their choice. 'Sensible and dignified' – an interesting choice of words, not mine but his, picked up somehow – implies, however, that they have had a chance to watch other people being sensible and dignified. And kind, and forgiving, and relaxed. The main thing children need from a family is that example. It is also one of the main things they need from a school, a childminder, a neighbourhood, and a whole society as reflected in the television screen. It is not always what they get.

7: Home Sweet Home?

Back in the 1950s when I was growing up, every women's magazine had a story about a happy housewife. It was probably reaction against the war years, when many women had to work in factories or in the services, and live in barracks or land-girl huts wondering whether their men would ever come home again; but the result was that the stories specialized in a sort of soft pornography of the Wendy house: a deliberate titillation of the nesting instinct. 'Laura sang happily as she whisked around her gay, neat little kitchen, enjoying the sunlight on the cheerful red curtains, and lovingly arranging her spick and span new plates on the dresser she and Ronnie had chosen together . . .' Laura was perfectly happy at home, like Mrs Tittlemouse, although naturally, to give the story a bit of drama, she would have some little problem – worrying about Ronnie seeming a bit distant, or whether she had spent too much on loose-covers. This was always resolved, not by going out for a walk together, or on holiday, but firmly within the wee bower itself: an embrace concluded the story, generally with a bit more titillating stuff about the 'bright modern wallpaper' perhaps framing Ronnie's manly head, or the cheerful brass fender winking merrily at their happiness.

The result of being raised on this stuff was, for me, an abiding sense of guilt at not feeling quite as keen as Laura on my little nest. I can do the bit with the bright curtains and winking brass for a little while, but the shine goes off it if I think I can't get out. And straw-polling amongst friends of all ages reveals a remarkable number of women, career as well as homebodies, who find the domestic interior less than totally thrilling. At this point I should confess that sometimes, in the summer, I sleep in a shed on wheels in the garden. A shepherd's hut, used on the farm at lambing-time and otherwise parked on the lawn. It is quite wonderful: a kind of very short camping holiday. There is nothing much in the shed apart from the bunk and a lantern and me and my paperback; I wake in the morning to a different world, with birds twittering instead of the boiler humming, and pad barefoot across the wet grass to the kitchen with considerable reluctance.

It is always a frightful moment. Sometimes there is nothing more claustrophobic than one's own family home. Wherever you look, there is something to be done. Curtains to hem. Letters to answer. Odd socks to rescue. Niffy trainers lying around. Phone messages to respond to. Complicated forms from the school. Cats to feed. People's precious stamp collections being chewed up by an escaped hamster behind the sofa. The sink-tidy overflowing with old teabags. Pictures you meant to hang eighteen months ago. Barely any room in the house does not carry its quota of accusing clutter, and on those summer mornings it takes iron self-control not to turn 180 degrees and flee back to the nice bare little hut.

Indeed, I have a friend, a mother of four, who loves nothing more than to go on holiday to Center Parcs, even though she has to self-cater in a villa. 'It's the joy,' she says, 'of having exactly six knives, forks, spoons and cups, and no more. Exactly what you need to get by, nothing lying around, just all clean and bare.'

Clutter

Clutter is a terrible domestic enemy. If you hate waste, and are always thinking things will come in handy, you will have kitchen drawers full of half-finished glue, ping-pong balls, cardboard photograph frames, clever machines for piercing the ends of eggs, boxes of clothes that you mean to take to the jumble, outgrown single shoes it would be a crime to throw away, pottery badges of villainous design, etc. If you are sentimental you will never throw away any artefact the children bring home from nursery school, and some of these are large, awkwardly shaped and, after five years or so, really rather pointless. The odd egg-box duck on the fridge is acceptable: the shoebox made into a combine-harvester with rather sucked-looking straws sticking out of it is, after a while, rubbish. Familiar and beloved rubbish, but nonetheless junk.

If you are maternal, you will keep all your old baby clothes just in case. If you are family-minded, you will keep horrid great bin-bags full of toddler clothes until your sister-in-law's baby gets big enough to have them forced on to its mother, willing or not. I know one woman who bombarded her sister-in-law with so many foul old clothes that in the end the victim took desperate action and stuffed a pouffe with them. One day, I predict, the pouffe will explode at the seams during a family gathering, acrylic dungarees will spill everywhere, and there will be a very, very painful scene. Finally, if you are one of those women who is always changing size, like me, then you will have dreadful hampers and cupboardsful of outmoded clothes which might a) fit you again one day and b) come back into fashion. Should I lose two stone this year, and psychedelic loon pants come back into fashion after twenty years, believe me, I shall be ready. Oh yes.

Some clutter is just a symptom of healthy, varied, relaxed family life. Nothing is more chilling than an utterly tidy house when you know that children live in it. They are generally TV addicts (a few parents positively encourage computer games because they make no mess. Creepy, I call it). But clutter can become a menace and an oppression, and the bigger your house is, the worse this clutter problem will be. Inhabitants of small houses do, in the end, find that common sense prevails over sentiment and miserliness, and get on the phone to a miniskip-hire firm. But the big house swallows everything, until like all indiscriminate gluttons it starts to feel unhealthy, blemished and depressing. Remind me to show you my cupboard under the stairs sometime.

There are two ways that mother, as Head of Tidiness in The Family PLC, can approach the problem (for mother, read father,

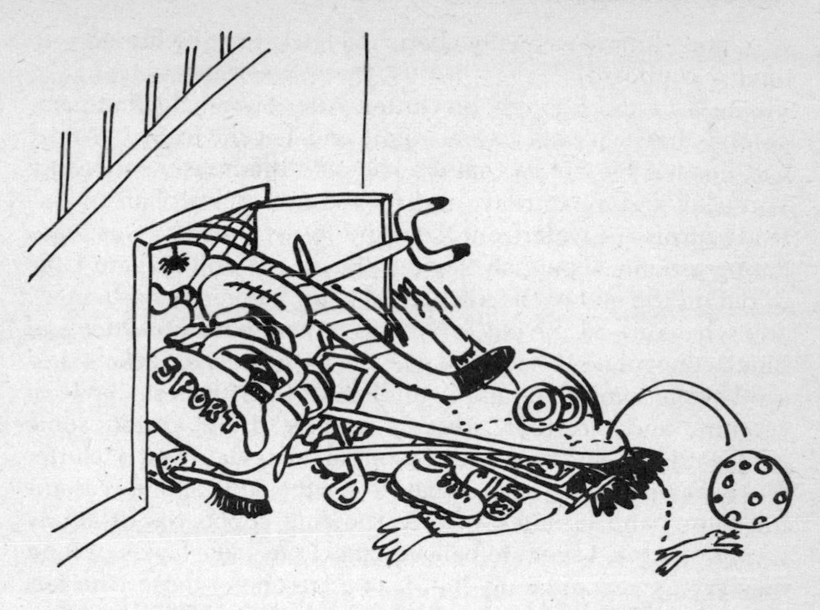

if you have that kind of father in the house). Either she (he) enlists the full help and co-operation of every single family member in selecting what will be thrown out. Or she (he) does it all in deadly secret while they are away, and never admits to having done anything at all. If you take the latter, ruthless course, you have to steel yourself to ignore all agonized cries of 'Where's my broken bit of toy tractor I use to prop up the corner of my fort?' and 'My old camouflage jacket! I love that jacket! It must have been stolen!'

But you must be consistent. Nothing brings out accusations of favouritism like throwing away one child's sacred cardboard box while sparing the other's collection of dead starfish, or tearing up a ten-year-old's beloved tracksuit trousers (worn well above the anklebone after two years) when you haven't the nerve to do the same to his teenage brother's repulsive tattered Heavy Metal T-shirt. And if Father's golf clubs are allowed to live in the lobby, and Mummy's exercise-bike blocks the landing, why must Jimmy's equally cherished cricket bat be hurled into the toy cupboard?

One last word, though, on clutter. After I wrote the first paragraphs above, it was late at night and I went to bed. And I had this terrible dream that we had sold the house, between a Thursday and a Saturday, and moved into a neat, bare, light, ready-furnished waterfront flat. And in my dream, I was wandering around hopelessly saying, 'But there isn't a spare table to put on the end of the kitchen table for big family parties . . . and where are all the old furry toys, where have Mr Otter and Blue Lion gone? What shall we do with the life jackets and sail-bags in winter? Where is my Father Christmas stockpile of eccentric and rare toys? There's no attic! Help! Quick, some cardboard boxes!' The sense of panic at being deprived of clutter woke me up, drenched in sweat, to see the familiar and reassuring lumps and bundles and overflowing cupboards of family life around me. I seem to believe that clutter, like layers of fond memory, is part of family life. If you are one of those who feel that way, I have only one bit of advice. Do NOT marry an ultra-tidy man. Or if you must, have separate sitting-rooms.

So when it comes to managing the constantly changing, shifting mass of objects a family attracts, there are two things to remember. High-flying, imperious executive parents should keep telling themselves that a family is not a training exercise or a challenge in time-management. Laid-back, hippyish, stay-at-home dreamy parents should keep telling themselves that actually, perhaps it is. In other words, you have to be enough of a ruthless, efficient manager and enough of a barker of orders to assure that the bicycles and cricket bats are under cover at summer dusks, that dirty clothes are in the dirty-basket and clean ones claimed from the ironing-board and put away. But also enough of a mother, or father, not to allow these matters to take priority over affection, sympathy, digestion, or a good family laugh.

If you achieve this latter aim, though, I fear, your house will end up looking like mine.

Moving house

This is, next to a major fire, quite the best way to get rid of clutter. Once we have seen it all in cardboard boxes out in the merciless light of day, even the worst of us squirrels are happy to abandon some of it for ever.

But moving house once you have a family is also a severe jolt. Single, or as a bachelor-couple without children, one seems able to indulge a moment's sentimental retrospective and then blithely move on, with little to fret about beyond rising damp, builders, wall coverings and kitchen fittings. Parenthood changes all that. If you don't believe me yet, just you wait until you have to leave the house where you brought home your first baby, stumbled through those sleepless nights, hung up a bouncing carrycot, saw those fat legs make their first steps and those big eyes fall on their first Christmas tree. Just you wait until you find yourself thinking that selling this, marketing it, being persuasive with agents and buyers, is almost a pornographic activity: like putting your daughter on the streets. You are pushing something from the very private side of life out into the public, financial domain. The very house-agent's brochure seems like lipstick on the whore; the contract of sale like a betrayal. Houses with children in become precious, far more rapidly than houses with only adults.

And wait until you take the last walk round when the removal men have gone, and find a matted old rabbit lying abandoned behind a radiator. Sniff. Even hardened Daddies get maudlin at this point. Even when all of you have been longing to move, and the move is upmarket and exciting: it hurts.

In the rush of moving, though, it is easy to forget that it probably bothers the children much more. Whatever they say, however much they wanted to move. Our first family move affected only the adults, because Nicholas was too small to know. But the second, eight years later, was fraught. Both children knew they could take their things, and would stay at the same school and have the same friends, but 'I can't take the fireplace, can I? We'll never sit by that fire again . . . and what about the beam in my bedroom that looks like a ship? Will my own curtain come, so the sun looks the same in the morning? Will the new bath have a mark like the old one?' If you are moving to somewhere bigger, or nicer, there is the adventure of the new house to hold out: if it is to the most inexperienced eye definitely a worse house or flat, or neighbourhood, they will need even more support. Just when you do, too.

I was much comforted in my most unwilling move – the one which bothered the children most – by watching a programme in the BBC *All our Children* series, in which a little girl called Cristina was taken from a violent home in the slums of Brasilia and put in an orphanage. She took her blue stuffed rabbit and her two precious dolls and, in the clean bleakness of the Lor Betel home, she looked after her three younger brothers and their treasures with determination. And she ranged her dolls on her bed each morning in exactly the same places. With these small duties and small icons Cristina created herself a new home, for a year. Then the cameras followed as she was moved seventy miles out of town to the orphanage's farm, where older children take a rapid and hardworking path to adulthood. Goodbye to the two smallest brothers, and to every remotely familiar urban vista. She packed the rabbit, the two dolls, a spare dress and a toothbrush, and that was it. She even sang on the bus. And six hours later – you are there before me – she unpacked her few possessions and ranged them with superstitious care on her new bunk. In the same order as ever. And she took to the new life, and became contented in time.

The brave, distant little girl on the screen was a salutary reminder of the resilience of children in any change of home, provided that their own household gods – whether water-pistols, china dogs or furry animals – are respected. Cristina made me more solicitous of my own children's possessions in the chaos of moving, more sympathetic to crazy theories about which way the bed should face and why the old curtains should be put up even though they did not fit. In the process, the removal men casually told me that one of the funniest aspects of house-moves is that people always want the furniture arranging in the living-room in the same way as in the old house – even though it patently doesn't fit the new-shaped room. Since we have these half-superstitious feelings about home objects, we might as well indulge them and revel in them, all together. And certainly not allow anyone's tatty old chair or dog-eared pony poster to become a cause of friction. To move into a fresh, newly-painted home and allow your children to make their corner of it look as messy as the old one is not a sign of weakness or bad housekeeping. It is a sign of love.

And children are much nicer than we give them credit for. In one family undergoing a divorce, the eleven-year-old girl and her thirteen-year-old brother had to leave a large garden, a swing in a big mulberry tree, a wilderness of fruit-bushes and a tree house for a town flat. They were not best pleased at the idea, although it had been very carefully sold to them as being close to school, close to friends, and highly suitable for the teenage lifestyles they were on the verge of. Still they sulked.

But two days before the move, their mother relates, the girl came to her with a request. She knew the buyers had younger children, and wanted to leave them a letter about the best parts of the house and garden, the dens and secret places she had grown up with. Her brother eventually decided to join in: together they produced a kind of will, leaving all the old pleasures to the next generation. It occupied all their time for the last two days, and they brought an astonishing passion to the job. Their mother weepily photocopied it before she left the letter to the new family, so precious was the testament. And, although the divorce was not of her choosing and contained a degree of bitterness, after a brief struggle she sent a copy to her husband, too: in memory of the times when family life had worked well, under the mulberry tree. If children could manage change with grace and generosity, so could she.

Territory

Every animal needs territory. Children who share bedrooms need a line across the floor, or private cupboards, or even a sacred box into which nobody else may go. Even bookshelves may have to be partitioned off, if that keeps the peace. And invasion of one another's territory – especially if it is not justified by a search for stolen property – is to be quite firmly discouraged (although a system we hit on quite by accident has worked remarkably well: one child is sole custodian and librarian of all cassette tapes in the house – speech or music – and has the responsibility of retrieving them when the car gets too full, or after a Walkman-dependent holiday trip. Anyone – including his parents – who wants a tape applies to the librarian, who opens the drawer with due ceremony, and permits them to take it. I would never have set this system up on purpose, but it seems to suit all our temperaments).

But parents need territory, too. Fathers tend to take it more readily than mothers: most households seem to have a Dad's chair, but fewer have a Mum's chair. Men are adept at organizing themselves workshops, studies, potting-sheds, corners of the garage where they potter about; women are modestly reluctant to take what Virginia Woolf identified as that great need, 'A room of one's own'. We stick to the kitchen, and the kitchen is always communal anyway, so we have nowhere. We ought to try, though: certainly it does no harm for the smallest children (and largest husbands) to have it made perfectly clear to them that some cupboards, some surfaces like the dressing-table, and even perhaps if you are lucky one room, is Mummy's Private Place. Sacred. Vestal. Not to be filled with one-eyed rubber Boglins, or raided for face-painting sessions, fancy dress, or components to make a showjumping course for the kitten. Again, the more you respect other people's territory, the more they ought to respect yours.

When it comes to teenagers' bedrooms, opinions vary. Some are in favour of ruthless, compulsory cleaning, either by the occupant or a parent. Others think that in order to mature properly, like a good wine, teenagers should be left alone in their squalor but not assisted to find things under the mess. I have not reached this stage yet (except with a nineteen-year-old resident nanny, whose room was spectacularly messy at all times), but on the whole, I favour the middle course. Which is to have a basic hygiene rule (no dirty underwear or socks, no cups and plates with mould on; any breach of this rule to be punished by a vicious, unprovoked clean-up which might, just might, also include the Heavy Metal posters).

One other word on teenagers and their rooms. There was a court case not long ago involving a boy computer hacker, and in court it emerged that at nineteen years old this boy had spent long hours, years almost, alone in his room with an old computer, fiddling with it, and 'never had a girlfriend'. There was much censorious muttering about this, and blaming of his mother (who seems to have tried very hard, even to the point of hiding his computer discs), and the fact that it was a computer he played with brought out all sorts of other technophobe dreads in society about computer addiction. But I found myself surprisingly strongly on the boy's side. I have a brother who at one stage, as a broke articled legal clerk, shut himself in his room in all his spare time, teaching himself the folk fiddle, accordion and tin-whistle off records on a decrepit turntable and seeing nobody. 'Well,' he remembers now, 'you are not a lovely creature at that stage, spotty and uncouth, you are in a chrysalis, you don't want to see anybody.' He emerged quite happily after a year or two, formed folk bands, got out, met friends, courted, got married: a little later than the more frenziedly social teenagers now considered 'normal', but after all, there was a time not long ago when no boy of nineteen was expected to have a girlfriend yet, for heaven's sake. Other teenagers I have known to shut themselves away alone just listening to music for unreasonable lengths of time; to read obsessively and hate all interruption, or to fiddle with motorbikes for hours. It seems that some adolescents are made to be outgoing and sociable and others – like a good wine, sometimes the more interesting ones

– need ages in the dark, uninterrupted, growing up at their own pace.

Our job as parents is not to dragoon them or interfere with the decor of their rooms. It is to watch out for signs of drugs or drink – which do need swift intervention – and otherwise merely to be respectfully on hand with hot food, should they deign to emerge for it. Yes, it is irritating. Very. But a decent modicum of peace and privacy can be traded – if necessary by written contract, as some psychologists suggest – for halfway reasonable behaviour at family gatherings and on holiday. Adolescents live in another country: as any international statesman will tell you, treaties work, with endless patience and persistence. Invasion of territory and martial law very rarely does.

8: He Ain't Tolerable, He's My Brother: Siblings

Victoria Gillick, that doughty and much-pilloried campaigner for moral and family values, is a mother of ten and one of my unexpected heroines. I say unexpected, because some of her robustly Catholic views on contraception and morality are not ones which I share. However, as a very cheerful, humorous, uncannily calm mother of ten children she is a gold mine of useful information about sibling politics. I grilled her on the subject once and she came up with several interesting – and rare – fruits of experience.

For a start, you have to understand what lies behind the utter rejection of contraception which she and Gordon Gillick have practised ('We wouldn't have given tuppence for the idea of sterilizing our healthy young bodies with chemicals, bits of metal or rubber. Clanking to bed was a turn-off'). It is not only a religious belief, but a curiously appealing philosophical one: of family life as a big rolling party, where anyone who happens along is welcome. The result of this, in the life of large families, is a kind of cheery fatalism: there you all are, and you might as well make the best of it. To have a really big family has its drawbacks, but it also makes for a kind of troopship camaraderie. Mrs Gillick reckons that the most difficult bit – worse than being pregnant for the eighth time, worse than twins, worse than having five under five and no inside lavatory, worse than mixing bread-dough in a baby bath or stretching half-a-pound of mince to feed ten – was the bit near the beginning when she only had two children. 'They bicker all the time,' she says. 'And if you've quarrelled with one sibling, you've quarrelled with all your generation. It's lonely and claustrophobic, at once.' Once the family starts to grow, she reckons, there is always one sibling to gang up with, always someone you are on good enough terms with to talk secrets. Relationships wax and wane, flourish and vary between the different ages: sub-teenagers can be very tender with toddlers, then grow away from the babies for a while, then return as old friends.

This is worth bearing in mind, not because most of us have the stamina, or can bear the financial terrors, of having vast families, but because it is a very important truth. Two children – which is starting to be the norm – is a very awkward number. They fit easily into a small car with both parents in front, but that is the best you can say of it. All siblings bicker at times, but a pigeon-pair, born within a couple of years of each other, can be atrocious company. Can drive you wild. In *How Not to Raise a Perfect Child* I dwelt on the snares of being obsessively fair, on possessions, mutual insults, fighting and the saintly qualities required of an arbitrator between quibbling siblings. One of the central rules was that nobody, ever, under any circumstances is allowed to hit anybody else with an instrument: whether it be toy, wooden spoon, shoe, or stick. Nor may any karate-chops be used, hair be pulled or eyes poked, whoever started it. This inhibition – which has to be drummed in from eighteen months old onwards – limits the actual physical damage. As a piece of advice, it also has the authentic ring of desperation which sets in during the first years of parenthood. But thinking now about the whole family perspective, and about older children and teenagers as well, there are some things to add.

First, never be surprised, or shocked, or disappointed, by how furious siblings can get with one another. Think how much married couples get on one another's nerves – and they chose each other, for heaven's sake. Siblings didn't. Nor can children defuse the tension by going to bed together, or getting drunk. They are stuck under the same roof, sometimes in the same bedroom: they know one another's annoying habits far too well. They know there is no chance whatsoever of divorce. So when they fight, they can really let rip in safety, and there is precious little to stop them.

Except you. At the point of greatest heat you can cry, 'Se-pa-

rate! Now! Glass wall!' or some such code to indicate that they must no longer touch one another or listen to a word the other says until they have cooled down. But that is only first aid. A better cure is only won by sitting down, and making each child state his or her case clearly, in turn, without hyperbole or abuse. Courtroom procedures have been tried, with some success, by legally minded parents: each child stating its grievance uninterrupted and accepting the decision of the court. Others resort to mere separation, and a withdrawal of all treats and sympathy until the protagonists have come to a reasonable settlement by themselves. The first system is probably better with siblings of unequal power and personality, and the second where they are genuinely well-matched.

But you have to do something. I did, at our own children's most warlike phase, wonder whether I was not making it worse by intervening in these dog-fights. Perhaps I should just walk away, or push them into a soundproof room and let nature take its course. In a calm moment, I asked them. They unanimously agreed that it was a parent's job to stop fights. 'Otherwise it would get worse, and worse, and Rose would end up in hospital from some of the things I've thought of doing to her,' said my son, quite seriously. 'And if you weren't ever stopped from fighting and made to be at least polite to each other when you were small, I think you'd fight madly with everyone for all your life.' He also, after more thought, said that he thinks that is probably 'how bullies start, like the ones you get at school, by practising on their brothers and sisters at home'.

I think he is probably right. Tempting though it is to embrace minimalist parenting and let nature take its course out of your hearing, intervention is a duty. Canvassing teenagers, they generally said that the idea of a court hearing, or at least a tribunal round the kitchen table with their parents actually listening to their case, would be the best solution. 'Because at least you'd know they were taking your feelings seriously, as if they mattered.' Some said it would be good if someone took notes. One member of a family of five, whose parents do hold tribunals, said that they generally end up in gales of laughter with the original grievance forgotten.

Prolonged animosity is worth looking at even more closely. Is one child jealous of another? If so, is there a hidden reason for this? Do you habitually take a different attitude over the same behaviour, depending which child it comes from? Is a daughter being short-changed compared to a son, her interests belittled and less supported than his? Or a son being made to feel a loutish outsider in a very feminine household? A pretty daughter, or sporty son, outshining a less conventionally gifted sibling of the same sex?

An aggrieved sense of difference can build up from the most absurd beginnings: I hated my elder brother for ages because he had been taken on a long train journey which I had missed and because everyone had laughed at me for being jealous. And my own daughter became seriously miffed at one stage because when she came down after bedtime, we abruptly chased her back to bed, whereas her brother got a more sympathetic reception. The reason for this was not that we are monsters, but that she had – all the previous year, at the age of six – driven us bananas with endless, mischievous, debilitating appearances up to five times every evening, and the sight of her after eight-thirty made us terrified it would start again, wrecking our only moments of peace in the day. Whereas the boy had never cried wolf, but only come when he needed help or reassurance quite badly; so we were kinder. What had happened was that she had stopped her annoying habit, and now came when she really needed us, and was apparently rejected, unreasonably. And he still wasn't on similar occasions. She raised the matter, being a forceful child; we saw her point, explained what had been bugging us, apologized and never snapped again. Well, not much, and equally at both of them. A small, stupid, embarrassing-to-relate episode: but entirely typical of the way jealousy can be fuelled by weary parents who fail to keep their eye on the ball and notice that a child has moved on to a new phase.

The pleasure of having a sibling, though, should never be underrated. Even the most stroppy, combative children are more often than not playing together, inventing private games, hauling one another outside and generally interacting. Parents can further this process by artfully introducing games which need two players at least, birthday presents of walkie-talkies, ping-pong tables and so forth; also by reading books aloud in the evening to all the children so that they have more and more common ground and common fantasy games to play.

Kindness between siblings is something you can positively promote, too, by encouraging it and praising it. You can insist on certain ground-rules over matters like private sweets and Easter eggs (to wit, *chez nous*, that nobody eats a treat in front of someone else without offering it round politely). You can send one child with good news for another (that you are all going to the cinema, or swimming), and generally work on their relationship with one another as much as you work on yours with them. All right, it takes time and thought: but so does breaking up fights.

Curiously, the most encouraging thing I ever encountered among siblings involved handicapped children. Linda Scotson, who recovered her son Doran from severe brain injury by intensive therapy, was helped by his elder sister Lili to an extent she thought remarkable – but discovered was quite common. In *The Other Child* – well worth reading for any family, whether it has a handicapped member or not – she describes Lili's ferocious determination to dress this stiff, hopeless baby, to play with him, drag him around and generally pull him into life. It is a pattern recognizable from the lives of handicapped children like the writer Christy Brown, who was trundled round Dublin in a handcart by a mob of brothers and sisters. Linda Scotson lauds the sibling contribution: 'Unrecognized, unsung, generally unrewarded,' she says, 'sibs do their best to bring hope and humanity into operation in a desperate situation. They hate deathliness and morbidity. They know you can never go back, you have to push on.'

The cases she writes about are extreme, but strangely, looking at families of healthy siblings, the same principle applies. They push one another, goad one another, keep things moving; they counteract depression and isolation, and they know a great deal about one another (even if most of it annoys them). Even my own warring pair have surprised me on occasion: Nicholas as a toddler yelling at the crying Rose to 'Shut up, stupid, you'll get your dinner in a minute!' – and Rose stopping, glaring at him, before they burst together into companionable laughter. Rose getting lost at Warkworth Castle (worst twenty minutes of my life) and Nicholas saying quietly, anxiously, concentratedly to me, 'Don't just call her, Mum. Stop and listen, in between, in case she answers.' Countless occasions when one of them has put out a hand – albeit a rough, grudging one in its manner – to help the other one. Or, on being given a small treat, demanded one for the sibling. Or put real thought into a birthday present and the keeping of the secret.

Brothers and sisters are magic: the magic can go sour, but if you practise careful family politics to ensure it does not go too sour, they have one another as a gift for life. For the years after you are gone.

9: Family Rules and Customs

One of the surest signs that you – a couple and some babies – are mutating into a genuine, full-grown family is that you start to develop family rules. A family rule is not one merely imposed on the children by the parents – such as 'No TV until after homework' – but one the parents also obey. Such as 'No Wellington boots in the kitchen', 'No swearing worse than "bloody"' or 'Anything left lying around on work-surfaces after 5 p.m. on Sunday gets binned'. Naturally, some apply more rigorously to children, particularly where the phone bill is concerned, but essentially they apply to everyone. And there is nothing children enjoy more than seeing their father made to wash his hands before a meal, or their mother reprimanded for breaking the rule about no-reading-at-table-except-the-breakfast-table.

Family rules are not oppressive, or dictatorial: they are just an affirmation of common standards (pretty low ones, in our case) and of the fact that we all have to live together. Myself, I don't mind mess: but there comes a point when mess gets in other people's way, preventing them from sitting down, doing homework, or finding a clean coffee cup. So there have to be rules and customs to keep mess in order. Again, we do not eat very formally: side plates and saucers are virtually unknown at our table. But we have a liking for conversation, and archaic ideas about family meals, so if a family meal is happening, a special dispensation is still required for anyone – anyone – to spend it with the television or radio on. This includes the TV farming weather forecast. And, alas, *The Archers*. If it so happens that we are all sitting down to supper at Archers time, either I have to crawl to the rest of them to be let off the rule just this once, or do without my daily fix of soap opera. It may sound silly, but it reaffirms the very important civilized idea that decent social behaviour is not something imposed by authority on the weakest, but something arrived at by consensus in a community. So there. And yes, they do sometimes ban me having my soap opera on, especially if I banned *Star Trek* the night before, and I sometimes miss it.

I straw-polled a collection of different families for typical family rules. The healthiest families seemed to have more of these communal rules than the tense, uptight ones, which was interesting. Here are a few:

- All outdoor shoes to be left at the back door when coming in from the garden
- All personal plates and cutlery to be cleared from the table when leaving it
- All trunk calls to be written on the pad, with appropriate timings (a houseful of teenagers, here)
- Bedtime is bedtime. Moreover, adult time begins at 7.30, after which large children may read quietly or play cards elsewhere, but disturb adults only for sensible reasons, or to kiss goodnight
- Everyone shall clean their teeth and sometimes wash
- And feed their own pet. Every time Mummy has to do it because they forgot, they are fined 10p pocket money
- No hamsters in the bathroom, ever. Not since the plughole incident
- No toys at the table
- No personal remarks before 9 a.m.
- Everyone shall apologize to everyone else if appropriate, and be friends again, before bedtime. Let not the sun go down on your wrath
- There is a cardboard box under the kitchen table. Things which should not be lying around will be thrown into it each evening during *The Archers*. On Friday night at 7.15 precisely it will be emptied into the nearest skip, with no right of appeal (this woman has thrown a remarkable variety of things away but only, she says, one precious item per person before the message sunk in)

- No item of clothing will be washed unless it is in the wash-basket. Clean clothes will be fetched by each person from the clean basket. Anyone failing to grasp this can go to school without socks. See if I care.
- No visitors to stay, of any age, without consulting or at least informing the rest of the family members in time for them to plan a getaway night of their own. This includes everyone, particularly in-laws, long-forgotten aunts, old schoolfriends, ex-boyfriends with their unknown new wives, and teenage cronies with personality problems.

You see what I mean? Some of these rules I think are quite good, some quite impracticable. It depends on your family. Do not fall into the common mistake of governments and set up unenforceable laws. This only leads to chaos. Few rules and reasonable ones work best.

Democracy

Creeps in gradually. There is no point asking a baby under three what he thinks the family should do for their annual holiday (not all that much point asking whether he wants pink or white ice cream, frankly). But as children get older they start to like the idea of having a say in family decisions. And by the time they reach their teens, if they have not been in the habit of getting such a say – or at least a voice in the family Parliament – they will be so fed up with being pushed around that they will rebel in pointless and anti-social ways.

Actually, they might anyway. But I am all for a bit of democracy. Start with the decisions which actually can be made either way, and don't matter overwhelmingly to you as Chairman of the Board (i.e. don't start with 'Darlings, do you think Mummy should get a part-time job?' when you know you've got to). And let them list the pros and cons of a situation, because it is good practice for life. You can sit down, even with a six-year-old, put on a serious expression and say 'Look – what do you think we should do? We could go swimming on the way to Granny's, but that would make us too late to watch *Star Trek* with her. Or we could go straight there and fit in swimming tomorrow, by having an early lunch.' They really like to be asked. It gives a sense of how to plan, and decide between alternatives, and make the best of a bad job. All are useful lessons. They also, by the time they are eight or nine, often have better ideas than you do because your managerial brain has become overtaxed. They might say, 'It doesn't matter missing *Star Trek*, because we could video it, and Granny doesn't like it anyway. Let's go swimming.'

The same principle applies to holidays – where there is a real choice – and even, a few years on, to schools. With many caveats ('Look, if you insist on St Bobbin's, we might not be able to afford the fees and a holiday as well', or 'The school run will be appalling if you choose Greenbridge High, and when you're twelve you'll have to take the bus on your own'), you can perhaps offer a choice between reasonable alternatives. This may not be possible: but if it is, just think of the pleasure and relief of being able to say to a child who grumbles about school, 'You helped choose it . . .' Early decision-making also leads to an early realization of one of the central, if rather depressing, truths of adult life: that 'as you make your bed, so shall you lie in it'.

Some parents become terrified that a modicum of family democracy will somehow 'spoil' children; but having too many rigid decisions taken for them will spoil them worse. Because they will then start disobeying and dodging round the rules because they are reasoning creatures and the rules seem unreasonable. Pre-empt this. Involve them in as much deciding as possible, birthday by birthday. It will pay.

Customs and Mores

This is a more flexible, and fascinating, area. Everyone remembers the first time they stayed with a schoolfriend's family, and how weird everything seemed ('They say grace!' or 'They all eat supper off trays' or 'Nobody is allowed even to say "bum"'. Or

'They all play music together in the evenings!'). Family jokes, family slang, even small details like the children being served first or last at table make a deep impression and create a new, often rather exciting, atmosphere. Indeed sometimes children fall hopelessly in love with other families, and as teenagers virtually live round at their friend's house because – for the moment – the way of life suits them better.

Manners

'Mind your manners. Don't talk when you're eating. Don't eat with your mouth open. Don't interrupt. Especially with your mouth full. Sit up straight. Show some respect for your elders, don't contradict, don't stare, don't make personal remarks. Or pick your nose. Or burp. Oh well, all right, you couldn't help the burp, but beg our pardon for it. No, it isn't the same as begging on the street. It's – oh, hell, it's traditional! Go on, say it. But not with your mouth full . . .'

Oh dear, oh dear. Is it any wonder the family meal is said to be on the way out, replaced by serial 'grazing' in which assorted gangling louts shamble into the kitchen at intervals during the day, stuffing lumps of frozen cholesterol into the microwave and spooning it into their vacant faces as they watch Australian TV soaps? Remember what a battleground the family meal can be, and you can see quite easily what is killing it off. It was – and in stalwart traditional families still is – the training-ground for good manners. It is the place where the new generation learns the code of behaviour which will take them through life as acceptable companions, colleagues and spouses. We do it ourselves whenever we can. Don't eat with your fingers, darling. At least, not the ice cream. Don't put your face into it, either.

The other traditional training ground for manners is public transport (unless you live where there is none, like us, and tend to go everywhere in the car, behaving like a cartful of pigs). On buses and trains the thoughtful parent may attempt to teach more lessons: don't jostle, dear. Don't get in that lady's way. Offer her your seat. Why? Because she's older than you and you should show respect. Gentlemen do offer seats to ladies (we are on dodgy ground here: the lady in question has a Walkman, two-metre hair extensions, and a T-shirt saying MEN SUCK. She is edging away from your bourgeois awfulness, not wishing to be classified as a poor old dear who needs a seat. Never mind).

On we go, to the party. Don't snatch. Don't stick your tongue out. Remember to say thank you for the nice time. You didn't have a nice time? Oh, of course you did! Thank Mrs Cooper . . .

Why do we do it? We live, after all, in an era where public life – press, politics, business, salesmanship – is constantly and horribly rude. Tabloid headlines scream UP YOURS, DELORS! and PADDY PANTSDOWN! Politicians sneer 'The honourable member's arguments are as flabby as his con-

victions'. Reviewers revel in insult, style writers jeer at whole sections of the population ('Essex men', 'Anoraks' etc.) Newspaper columnists are cheerfully prepared to bring in their victims' stammers, halitosis, big bums and failed marriages as factors in quite unconnected arguments. Advertisers ask, 'Are you sure your laundry isn't full of tell-tale odours?' and enjoy reminding you that you might die tomorrow, uninsured. It is a dreadfully rude age. So why not throw in the sponge, train our children in grabbing and abuse and devil-take-the-hindmost, and let them grow up throwing bones across the table and expressing their innermost feelings – the way we dare not do – when rung up in the bath by irritating acquaintances?

Because it would be so cruel, that's why. Next time you get sick of listening to yourself nagging about manners, think of the fate of those who have none. People think unmannerly children and teenagers are ghastly. They write them off. Human beings have to learn to be acceptable, not embarrassing or annoying to be with. Children have to learn, full stop.

But you can take a minimalist approach to manners. The days are gone when people got drummed out of polite society for drinking out of the finger-bowls. As long as children know that in company they use knives and forks properly, they can occasionally eat with their fingers at home. A few habits have to be kept up: such as eating with your mouth shut; but it is remarkably easy to convince a child of any age to do this simply by sitting opposite them yourself and masticating horribly with your mouth open. Or putting a mirror up while they do it. It also helps to borrow a really unpleasant, grabby, whining, rude child from another family (don't tell them why, of course) in order to impress on your own children that taking turns, passing things politely, listening to other people and sharing the last roast potato are aspects of human behaviour which are sorely missed when they are absent.

One other thing. Obvious though it may sound, it needs saying that if you are not polite to one another, and to your children, any manners you teach them by rote will not sink in very far, or survive any moments of stress. If you keep barking 'hurry up, hurry up' when they are doing something unhurryable, like going to the lavatory; if you criticize their clothes all the time, are abrupt with their friends, and snatch things off them; if you never say 'good morning' or ask how they slept, or how their day was – why should they? If you, the parents, snap at one another constantly, belittle each other's efforts in public and let slip remarks like 'Your father is a selfish moron', more than their emotional security will be undermined. Their manners will, too.

On the other hand, if you do let your own manners slip occasionally under stress, that is another valuable lesson for the young, interested onlookers. Because you can apologize for it, can't you? And then they find out about apologies, as well. As in: 'Alice, I am terribly sorry I called you a revolting child. I now realize it was not your roller-skate I fell over on the stairs but Daddy's sailing boots. It was dark, and Daddy had forgotten to change the lightbulb when I asked him. Daddy is a careless berk. No, I didn't mean that. I'm sorry. It was rude and vulgar. It's just that my knee really hurts. Sorry. Sorry everyone.'

With luck, they will make Daddy apologize properly too, when he gets back from the pub.

Family Modesty

When I was a child, I would occasionally spend the night with another family. They were the progressive sort: always having very upfront conversations about vaginas, and answering the children's questions with a fearful directness. Modesty was unheard-of: not only did the children throw off their clothes at random all over the house, right up to the late teen years, but the middle-aged parents roamed stark naked between bedroom and bathroom and joined us to watch *Z Cars* with their dressing-gowns hanging negligently open and various unspeakable bits reflecting, I remember, rather eerily in the screen.

I was very impressed, but possibly not for the reason they would have liked. It was just that we never had central heating in our house. So, *chez* Purves, one got dressed either under the bedclothes or in the airing-cupboard. Nudity was possible in the bathroom, but only if you switched on the overhead bar heater for about forty-five minutes first. Taking your clothes off was a major decision for eight months of the year at least, so if our parents had read the post-Freudian, progressive childrearing books of the time, and decided that it was necessary for us to see them naked in order to dispel castration anxieties, it would have been quite a performance. You can just imagine it: 'Now children, we are all going to be spontaneous and unashamed. Nip upstairs and turn on the bathroom heater for half an hour.'

Times move on. I suppose that the reticence of my parents and the bum-flashing of my friend's family represented the two factions which have been at war this century over the issue of family modesty. There was an era when most children's only glimpse of adult physiology was on the washing line. 'Cor Mum! Do they really fill up those big hammocks?' 'Shush, child, or you'll end up like your Uncle Arthur, who we never mention!' Modesty extended to oneself: convent girls of Sonia Orwell's generation had, she remembered, to bathe in long white robes; and convent girls of mine were told not to play the radio in the bathroom because it was unseemly for a man's voice to be heard in a room in which a pure young girl was stripped. (I have told many veteran male radio hosts this to cheer them up, and they are genuinely thrilled to have been considered such a menace.)

Then came the gurus of utter openness, like my friends' parents in the Sixties, who wanted to share everything about their physique with their children, discussed homosexuality at breakfast-time, and who also – come to think of it – were the type who put their thirteen-year-old daughters on the early high-oestrogen contraceptive pill, complete with side-effects, 'just in case'. Then there were compromisers, who felt that before the age of six (when children are deemed to go through their early sexual phase) family nudity was vital to ensure their future uninhibitedness, but that after six (when they enter every parent's favourite phase, of not giving a damn about any of it) one could pull one's wrapper shut again with a thankful sigh of relief. So gradually, we have all devised codes of common sense and expediency.

Instinct probably gets it right. Once the glorious immodesties of birth and breastfeeding are over, and when the penultimate toddler has had a last listen to Mummy's Amazing Kicking Bellybutton, most of us are only too thankful to retire behind a stout winceyette nightdress, permitting our offspring only casual and fortuitous glimpses of breast and bum. Dear old Dr Spock caused many sighs of relief when he discarded the extreme post-Freudian view and observed that, actually, the sight of great big naked hairy parents could upset children, and that they should keep reasonably covered up and have 'some privacy in the bathroom or toilet'. Purists may scoff at that, citing the meaningful conversations they have had with their little sons over the Tampax applicator. If you don't believe such purists exist, just read the relevant chapter in *Talking to Children about Things that Matter* by Sheila and Celia Kitzinger, and find out how the other half raps. My principal feeling after reading it was that, unlike thoroughly modern mothers, I would not be thrilled by the sight of my son running round waving a dear little white cotton-wool mousie like Mum sticks in her bum. I would probably be furious because, the odds are, it is the last one in the house.

There is actually a serious lesson to be conveyed by a modicum of parental modesty. Few would argue in favour of strict, prudish concealment in front of children but, at the same time, it does no harm to point out the essential truth that 'Bottoms are private!' This is one of the central protections a child has against sexual abuse, either by adults or (more likely) other children. They need to get the idea that, whereas there is nothing naughty about the bit between waist and knees, it is a bit which you are entitled to keep private if you want to. Parents, nurses and doctors should not rudely invade this area without explaining and asking permission, even to wash or examine it. Other children have no right to pull your shorts down for fun. Tickling under the arms is OK in a wrestling match, but under the legs probably isn't. And so forth. It follows that if your own small bum is private, then it is fair enough that Mummy does not want you bursting in when she is on the lavatory, or if Daddy hauls a flannel modestly over his floating bits when you come into the bathroom for a chat. The odd glimpse, followed by a fair answer to the question 'Why are you so hairy?' is one thing. But being constantly available as a life-size teaching aid for your children is quite another.

Besides, not all of us are as perfect as the diagrams in sex-education books. One father sums up his attitude by saying that his children are allowed to see him naked until the first time they say 'Yuck! Look at your flabby bum!' Whereon he starts hiding, for fear of further ridicule. I suppose you could be very hip and New Age, and argue that Dad ought to show them even more flabby bits, thighs, the lot, so that they learn 'to reject the hollow, shallow worship of physical perfection and accept the full human form'. But this one's eight-year-old has a particularly piercing line in scorn, and I wouldn't wish such a start to the day on anyone. Myself, I started turning my back to put on a bra when the youngest observed that my nipples looked like – no, I can't bring myself to type it.

Which brings us to the painful subject of teenagers. Teenagers, as everyone knows, are extremely modest. Prior to leaving the house in skin-tight leggings and tattered shirts tied under the bosom to reveal as much midriff as possible, or crotch-strangling jeans and bare chest for boys, they will hide in the bathroom for hours with the door locked, trying to will away their spots. Girls over eleven are not amused by siblings' attempts to ping their bra-straps or make comments on their very personal development. Nor are strapping great boys willing to let their misguided Mummies supervise bathtime. Wise parents respect this modesty, and impose it firmly on younger brothers and sisters. Who should not, it goes without saying, be included either in those confidential conversations about the Pill, the sleepover at Brian's parents' house while they are away, or the fact that the latest busty little hussy brought home by the son of the house is not sixteen at all, indeed not a day over fifteen, because you personally lent her Mum – your oldest friend – the family carrycot to bring her home from hospital in, it seems only yesterday . . .

But however tolerant parents are of teenage modesty, they are not rewarded by equal toleration of their own sloppy code of domestic behaviour. Far from wanting to accept their parents as sexual beings, teenagers would very much rather the wrinklies kept buttoned up, day and night, never laying a finger on one another except, perhaps, to knock off a wasp.

Teenage children of divorced parents are notoriously repelled and disgusted by the canoodling of a parent who has suddenly turned into a lover. Many a novel and memoir includes furious recollections of such things. But once puberty strikes, kids hate their natural parents cuddling, too. I suppose it is because sex, in the adolescent, is such an ungovernable and terrifying force that it is difficult for them to accept just how comfortably routine, how undramatic, a long-married couple can get. And that if your Dad puts his hand on your mother's bum for a moment, he is not actually feeling the same wild surge of adrenaline and testosterone as you did when you brushed past buxom Suzy in the science cupboard yesterday. This revulsion at parental sexuality was never more graphically expressed than by good old Hamlet himself: remember? 'Frailty, thy name is woman! . . . Oh God, a beast, that wants discourse of reason/Would have mourn'd longer . . .' Happy, giggling, newly-wooed mothers, however much they deserve some happiness after widowhood or divorce, would do well to remember Hamlet and be very, very discreet.

But it is not just sex which makes teenagers so dislike parental exposure. It is what Anna Ford used to call 'Body Fascism'. One teenage girl said frankly, 'I would honestly die if my friends ever saw the way my Mum's midriff hangs over her skirt before she puts her sweater on.' A boy says, 'My Dad's beer belly is just gross. It's as if that's where he keeps all his backward ideas about everything, all wrapped up in flab.' So can you blame Dad if he keeps it pulled in and buttoned up, and waits patiently for his son to grow old enough to realize that flat muscular tummies are not everything? If I were him, I would turn the heating down until the children leave home. This would have the added advantage to his peace of mind of stopping their disturbingly pneumatic girlfriends from ever taking off their sagging ribbed sweaters, or from wearing shorts.

But there is always revenge against these scornful, skinny, beloved creatures if you really can't stand their scrutiny. In the family which produced the above remarks, there is a Bohemian granny. They have a rather grand swimming pool, and Granny turns up at their house in summer and strips off to her wrinkled dugs to plunge nude into the pool and then stretch topless beside it, dreaming of bygone days with toyboys at the Venice Lido. The parents, themselves cautiously concealed against their children's contempt inside maximum-control Lycra swimwear and thick towelling gowns, know what to do. They bide their time, then send Sarah and Simon out, all unsuspecting, with Granny's cup of tea . . .

Technology: telephones and television

Technology has been ruining family manners ever since the invention of the telephone first caused parents to break off in mid-conversation with their children or each other, in order to answer a bell tinkled impertinently by some total stranger. Or tradesman. Or wrong number. In the early days of the telephone, grandees would get their butler to answer it, and bring the resulting message to them in the usual soft-footed, apologetic manner. Now, however, a telephone call is the equivalent of having a visitor burst in unannounced, ringing a bell, during your most private family moments. Do not expect young children to appreciate that a phone must be answered. If you don't have an answerphone device, at least apologize to them, and if the moment is fraught – for instance, if you are finally getting the story of who bullied your child at school – get rid of the caller, sharpish.

This is, of course, a counsel of perfection. But I do not apologize for offering it because I have annoyed my own family so badly in this way in the past that I would not wish it on any other. Working at home, for a number of demanding employers with tight deadlines, I have watched the fury of my children building up over the years about telephone calls. They both actively dislike the instrument; it takes their parents away from them into long incomprehensible grown-up business conversations; it is allowed to interrupt them, but they are not allowed to interrupt it. It ruins the rhythm of family life. Now we often leave the answering machine on, and wait to see who is calling and whether we really need to speak to them now. It is extraordinarily difficult, because it seems so arrogant to ignore a phone: but once you accept that it is arrogance on behalf of your family, not yourself as an individual, it becomes easier to practise.

Two other technological advances have altered family life. I do not count the microwave oven because I refuse to join the sanctimonious chorus about the demise of family mealtimes. How you cook, and whether you eat together or graze, is up to your own judgement and the shape of the day. More important are the television and the computer.

How to handle television is one of the great dilemmas of the age. On the one hand it is a window on the world, children learn from it, are entertained by it, and if they are watching it they are at least not out throwing bricks through neighbours' windows. On the other hand, since the average British child allegedly watches five hours a day, since some doctors are actively worrying about the lethargy it breeds in children, and since even the Princess of Wales has started preaching at us about it, the TV habit has clearly got out of hand. In the last book (*How Not to Raise a Perfect Child*) I suggested various habits to make the television a positive force, rather than a negative one. Choose programmes carefully, switch off at the end rather than waiting to see what comes next, foster a critical attitude, discuss programmes afterwards, never have it on in the background with the sound off, and ration (rather than ban) utterly brainless programmes so that everyone (including you) is entitled to one or two shameless lapses every week.

But in a family context, and the context of teenagers as well as young children, the problem becomes more complex. For one thing, children who stay up later are going to find out what they never knew while they were little – that their parents slump brainlessly and uncritically in front of the box more often than they would like to admit. For another, genuine family viewing – with everybody sharing and cat-calling and laughing and gasping together – becomes a real option. The conversations and

jokes and arguments arising out of a good film, comedy, or documentary can keep you all going for weeks. They can also provide, without undue effort or such American earnestnesses as self-conscious 'family co-counselling' or 'quality communication time', a very valuable set of clues as to what children think about human relationships, moral values, and sex. I always find it rather heartening when in the middle of an Agatha Christie mystery or a frivolous James Bond film, one of the children suddenly says, 'That's really gross. Bad taste. It's not showing respect for someone's death.' Or when they watch an adult row in a situation comedy with narrowed eyes and then pronounce, 'They're both being really, really bossy and stupid, aren't they?' I cannot see television, in this context, as being the fearful menace some commentators would have it be.

But growing children will also want to watch certain

programmes which you allow but which, with the best will in the world, you cannot face sharing with them. It could be football, or some computer-game quiz, or a brainless (but not particularly violent) cop series. In this case, if the children are under eighteen you ought to know something about the programme: dip into it, ask friends, check a film's rating. And you ought to know that they are watching, and in a general way, ration the time that they do so. Not necessarily to a strict hour-a-day, but so as to keep the average down. 'You watched four hours yesterday. Let's leave it off. You can video something for the next wet day if you want' is more reasonable than 'Switch that rubbish off and get some fresh air!' What that ration is you must judge, and agree, as a family. Possibly even with a bit of democracy involved. I cannot prescribe for anyone else. All I can remark is that it will be easier to ration television if your living area is not arranged exclusively around it: if, for example, there is a chair you can put in front of the screen looking inwards to a table where you sometimes play a family game of cards, or where someone sits and reads. If a room looks like a small cinema, that is how it will be treated.

Here, though, unashamedly, is a fierce personal prejudice. I think individual televisions in people's bedrooms are a very, very, very bad idea until the people concerned are at least sixteen. You do not have to give in to blackmailing remarks along the lines that 'all their friends' have them. It is a lie, anyway. Or if not, their friends need looking at.

Videos

We are bombarded with warnings about the vile, horrible, sadistic, sexually explicit films children can get hold of from video shops (or, indeed, off satellite channels). Our paranoia on this subject is aggravated by people telling us that they'll see them round at friends' houses anyway, so they cannot be protected.

Nobody should ignore these warnings, but nobody should overreact either. Once a child is at secondary school age, eleven and over, it is certainly hard to police what they see at friends' houses. You can make it quite clear to other parents that you prefer them not to have contact with anything carrying a higher certificate than their age, but other parents may not be at home, or frankly may not care.

The child's best defence against this tacky world lies within itself. If they have watched films and television with you, discussed levels of violence and sadism and immodesty, and been helped to consider why people make these things and whether it is really so clever to be taken in by them, they will have that defence. A child of eight is a natural leftie, and a natural satirist: quite capable of laughing with proper contempt at the fact that people in Hollywood and elsewhere are making huge fortunes out of filming other people's naked bottoms, or making actors pretend to pull other actors' innards out. Don't let the fantasy world draw them right in: analyse it, laugh with them at it. My children were desperate to see *Terminator* 2, which I had heard was extremely violent but not overly disgusting, since most of the violence was between one robot and another. In the end I watched it with them, we freeze-framed the special effects and the brilliant 'morphing' where floors turn into molten metal men and then into menacing humans. We discussed which bits were genuinely nasty, exploiting our fears and showing little respect for human beings, and which were clever and fun. Reading that back, it sounds appallingly sanctimonious and boring, but there were actually a lot of laughs in it. I do a really, really good Arnie Schwarzenegger impression. *Hasta la vista*, baby.

Children must know, above all, that there is no shame or wimpishness involved in refusing to watch really nasty videos, walking away, or expressing their view that a particular film is silly, unpleasant and perverted. Self-confidence helps; and so does knowing, quite clearly and happily from the family background and family viewing, that there is a better way to use a camera and a script. If, together, you have loved watching things which are wholesome, fun, true and inspiring – and that includes thrillers with a moral core and restrainedly handled violence – you are better able, even at ten years old, to reject those which are tiresomely tacky and exploitative and leave a bad taste in the mouth. The children we read about in the shock-horror tabloids, the ones who become addicted to extreme violence, sexual explicitness and morbidity, are generally those who have never learnt to enjoy anything else. And who have been alone too much with televisions.

And do not worry unduly about phases in which young teenagers watch moderately sexy (i.e. not hard porn) films with a terrible obsessiveness. They are trying to work it all out. Your best contribution is not to shriek in horror and take the plug off the machine, but to hire some irresistible and more romantic love stories on video. Even the most sex-obsessed teenagers can get carried away by Olivier's *Wuthering Heights*, or the bittersweetness of *Truly, Madly, Deeply*. If the general atmosphere of the family, the small world closest to them, is healthy, balanced and loving; if enough time is spent talking and laughing with real, three-dimensional people, it will be hard for mere videotape to corrupt them sexually either.

I suppose all this may sound laughably naive and idealistic. But simple ideals are often the best way to counteract complicated decadence. And while, undoubtedly, times will come when you have to say, 'No, you are not going to watch *Driller Thriller Killer Sex Machine III*. And that is that. Go to bed,' those moments will be much easier if you have taken a broad-minded view at other times.

Computer games

Computers help us, fascinate us, and occasionally scare us. One of the most recent spooky sci-fi scenarios concerns children and the chip, and the possibility – taken very seriously in some quarters – of the developing psyche being warped by dependence on computer games. In other words, Aaaagh! Is Sonic the Hedgehog stealing my little one's soul? Will Mario give him epileptic fits?

Sinister television documentaries have particular power to put the wind up us: I remember one which showed children learning from babyhood to play with bleeping, reactive, computerized toys, playing games for hours, and interacting better with the school computer than with their teacher. It showed how, in one quick stroll through a toyshop, you can find a machine to talk to your baby, one to tell it a story or sing it a lullaby, a computer to teach a toddler its first words, a jovial chatting red box to run through spelling with older children ('That is correct! Now spell – beau-ty!') And, of course, a computer game cassette to satisfy every violent fantasy.

Adult computer addicts are familiar figures (often rather rich ones, too, let it be said: think of 'Supernerd' Bill Gates of Micro-Soft, or those whizz-kids who make millions designing computer games). But the idea of a child, or a fresh-faced teenager, living in the glimmer of a VDU is somehow more repellent. Your own child, flicking through the levels of The Legend of Zelda, may seem contented and normal to you, but when dire tabloid warnings go out about epilepsy, and therapists warn – as one recently did – 'These are children with few friends, afraid of the give-and-take of conversation. Children who get their own way too much and have a short attention span for everything except the screen. Often they are children desensitized to violence by playing violent games,' then you get nervous. And cause a dreadful row by switching off the computer game in the middle of a crucial level, and get branded as a stupid bossy old Mum or gross, out-of-touch Dad.

Don't. Stay balanced. Look at the real situation in front of you, not some crisis from the extremes of society. When you actually go into some of the cases of 'computer game addiction' you will tend to find several other things are out of balance. It may be one departed parent and one bitter, upset, heartbroken one, creating an outside world considerably less enjoyable than Super Mario's bouncing adventures. It may be a shortage of friends, because of an unhappy school life or merely the parents' preoccupation with their own work and life and unwillingness to make the effort to mix the child (usually a boy between nine and eleven, initially) with other children. It may be lack of space and chance to do anything else, in a highrise city flat. It may be parents who – as the same therapist admitted – have simply 'forgotten how to be parents, or don't have the confidence. I wish they'd start noticing and worrying about what is happening a bit sooner, and not wait for the child to be playing thirty-five hours a week. If my child read for that long, alone, I would worry, wouldn't you?'

All these things need sorting out: but they are not the fault of the computer games. It is a fact that some computer games are disgustingly violent – and you should have no trouble banning them in your house if you allow other, more reasonable ones – and it is also a fact that computer games can be almost addictively fascinating. They offer you just enough chance to win, and learn new routes and skills, without ever making you feel you have quite mastered them. When my son first sucked us into this world, I used to sneak downstairs from my study while he was at school and play Mario until my head was spinning. Bowser the dragon always used to get me in the end.

But the novelty wore off. After a few days I no longer played till my head ached (longer than I had ever let the children play), and hardly ever bothered unless there was a new game, or something I half wanted to listen to on the radio at the same time. And the experience of having fallen for the games, then slacked off, enabled me to watch my children doing the same. You could always tell when my son, in particular, was unhappy or stressed at school: he played far too long and too intensely, becoming angry and snappish. Then I would usually intervene. When he was otherwise happy, he would do a few levels, 'save' the game, and stop.

Because the set lives in the corner of the kitchen, the convention is that the children play the games most of the time with the sound off. Occasionally we let them put it on, but as a general rule I find the absence of booms and crashes and bleeps helps to keep the emotional temperature down. The general conversation, or the radio, or the cat mewing for its tea reminds them there is a real world out there. The games become sociable: when parents drift by, saying, 'Ooh, look, you've won Yoshi the Dinosaur!', or friends and siblings sit round cheering the player on, computer gaming seems no more than another amusing indoor pastime. Some games – like SimCity, where you learn town planning and have arguments with your friends about where to site the power station – are so educational they bring a tear of pride to a parent's eye. I love sitting reading the paper while three children shout 'Look – if you install an urban monorail, you'll have to raise the taxes! And you can't get much unless you put another industrial zone in, can you?' Whatever the game, they drop it after a while – or when I start grizzling about the sun being wasted in the garden – and run out quite willingly. Sometimes they switch off of their own accord.

We have had few violent games. I accidentally let in Robocop, with its muggers and pit bull terriers, but the effect of parents, babysitters, and visitors drifting past the screen saying 'Oh, yuck, poor dogs, why do you have to keep punching and shooting them?' quite quickly made the children laugh the whole thing off. If the game had been tucked away in a bedroom, they might not have. In the end they decided the game was not technically as interesting as others, and swapped it.

But the best safeguard against computer addiction was a visit, one weekend, from a truly – if, I hope, temporarily – addicted little boy a bit older than them. He had every reason to seek electronic solace, with quite a few real-life problems to contend with; and my own children viewed his desperate, full-time determination to play with a sort of kindly dismay, and talked about it for weeks, relating it perfectly clearly (at the ages of eight and ten) to his other unhappinesses.

This is one family's experience – so far – and it is not intended to sound smug. I only think it worth describing as a counterweight to the often hysterical condemnation of all computer games and pursuits. We do set personal limits on the time they play, and the amount of time they have the sound on. We do – as with ordinary television – hold out resolutely against having sets in bedrooms, where a child can retire and isolate himself (it usually is a him) from the rest of life. And I set my face early on, and firmly, against the handheld portable 'Game Boy' type of game. They are harder to share, cannot be wonderful for even young eyesight, and most important of all, they stop children looking around at the outside world. There are few things more depressing than crossing the Channel on a ferry on a sparkling blue day, when children should be looking over the rail in wonder, or running around the decks annoying people, to see scores of them hunched obsessively over their little plastic boxes. Individual handheld computer games, the cheap kind, are less pernicious (especially on holiday) because you soon get fed up with them. To have the full power and inventiveness of a big-scale computer game with you at all times is a different matter. A case for parental veto or rationing, if ever there was one.

But there you are, you see: that is what I think, and what I do. Those are our family's own limits, right now, in this year of grace 1994. You may think differently. We may, in a year or two. But the point about all these new techno-problems is the same: as long as you are seeing clearly, thinking calmly, and looking at the actual family in front of you rather than some imaginary perfect (or equally imaginary doomed 'n' desperate) version, then you can come to a balanced solution. Next time a scare story comes up, take a deep breath, and think: few pastimes are all good or all bad; but I see few scare stories about cricket addiction, or cub-scout dependency syndrome. Keep cool.

10: Relative Values: The Wider Family

Why bother?

Remember Charles Darwin brooding on marriage, and how worried he was about the business of relatives? 'Forced to visit and receive relations but terrible waste of time . . .' He has a lot of sympathizers. Sometimes new couples blindly, unkindly, but rather bravely discard the tribes they came from. Sometimes they have to, because on religious, racial or class grounds the tribe is being so foully bigoted about the marriage. But sometimes they do it out of sheer thoughtlessness: moving away, striking out into the wider world together, starting anew. As the Bible says, they leave father and mother, sisters and brothers to cleave to one another and start a new family altogether.

I notice that I have already, musing about coupledom, rather praised this attitude and advised in-laws to keep out of the way for a while in early marriage. But with the birth of children comes a time when it is healthy – even pleasant – to let the tribe creep forward again and surround the new family with its old echoes. In other words, however decrepit your family tree looks to you, don't be too cavalier about chopping off the branch you sit on. When you start to be a family, the one which was there already turns out to have all sorts of unsuspected advantages. Yes, and problems.

Mothers-in-law

Now my mother-in-law, my mother-in-law, I'm not saying she's a difficult woman, but when she comes round our house, the mice start to throw themselves on the traps. Mind you, she always comes to us for Christmas. Every year for thirty years.

This year we're doing something different – we're going to let her in. I'm not saying she's fat, mind, but her knickers . . .

Stop, stop. We all know about mother-in-law jokes. Men have been sounding off for years about the wife's mother: they pose as victims of this tyrannical woman with her huge bloomers and invincible authority. Yet if you look at real life, what is the truth of the matter? That very few husbands are really at loggerheads with their mothers-in-law, and that many of them actually get on insultingly well with their brides' mothers, flirting outrageously and praising their cooking to the skies (much to the annoyance of their working wives).

It may wear a bit thin at times, this relationship, but on the whole men don't seem to suffer much, although they do tell the jokes. Whereas women – who really are quite likely to suffer persecution for their temerity in carrying off Mummy's best baby boy – never seem to tell mother-in-law jokes at all. Perhaps because it is all too serious. Extended family life is a delicate thing at the best of times; the relationship between a girl and her man's mother can be as fragile as spun sugar. Not one woman I talked to on the subject, even the most praiseful, was willing to have her real name put in print.

The reason we all started talking about it and plunging anecdotally into wonderful case-histories was that a few years ago, the then Prime Minister of Britain, Mrs Thatcher, took on a new and even sterner role when her son Mark led Diane Burgdorf up the aisle. Imagine! we all said. The Iron Lady as a mother-in-law! Poor girl!

But then we realized that this was a very simplistic reaction. In fact there are probably several distinct advantages in having a Prime Minister as your husband's mother. Many standard problems of the relationship are unlikely to crop up. For one thing, Prime Ministers are extremely busy, and a fully occupied mother-in-law is an excellent insurance against friction. It was never likely that Mrs Thatcher would find time – as one fond mother did for the first two years of marriage – to pop round every Monday and collect her son's shirts and underwear. 'I am not a proud housewife,' said the daughter-in-law of this particular laundroholic. 'And I wouldn't actually have minded, if the old bag had taken my things, too. But she never did.' Nor was Mrs Thatcher, an ocean away, likely to turn up too often for the ordeal of the Young Couple's Dinner Party, we thought, thus sparing them the bit with the stony-hearted potatoes or the garlic allergy or the 'Packet stuffing? How amusing!' bit.

On the other hand, we all mused, Mr Thatcher's bride would have a lot to live up to. If you marry a man whose mother is a legend of efficiency and energy, and only sleeps four hours a night, your husband will have certain expectations of what women can cope with. Any girl who has married the son of a 'Wonderful Woman' knows that it can be tough going.

Take Chloe, a brightish, prettyish, pleasant young teacher. Her house is not squalid (although the curtains have not been hemmed in the nine months she has lived there), her career is reasonable, although she will never be a headmistress; and her appearance is good enough for her husband Edward and her three-month-old son. So he says. However, his mother is a famous beauty, head of her own international business, and has created a house which has featured in glossy magazines as a classic interior. The needlepoint cushions were of her own making, the colour schemes and fabrics designed entirely by herself. 'It relaxes me when I'm travelling on business,' she murmurs. This woman has great charm, her three sons adore her; but Chloe finds that the very sight of Edward's wonderful, wonderful mother unnerves her so much that her tights go into ladders from the tense clenching of her toes. Not only is she younger and poorer and less experienced in life than her mother-in-law, but she knows she always will be. Her mother-in-law is oblivious to all this, luckily: once a strong woman finds out that her son's wife dislikes and fears her, she may turn nasty. 'Both my boys have married white mice,' said a tough old bat to me once. 'Nasty, small-minded, suburban little white mice. I don't bother speaking to them any more. Just chuck 'em a piece of cheese in the corner and get the news from my boys.'

The curious thing about relationships like this is how often the sons concerned entirely fail to notice that their wife has been written off. Even when she tells them. I once spent a weekend at his home with a boyfriend whose mother clearly could not stand the sight of me and was crushingly and consistently rude. When I pointed this out to him, he actually smiled and said, 'Oh yes, mother's such a marvellous character, everyone loves her for it, she's a real individual, speaks her mind.' End of romance, not before time.

In fact, men can be their own family's worst enemy when it comes to spotting the danger signs in relationships like this. Eric, who is now divorced, admits that when his young wife was grappling with a four-year-old, a baby, a part-time job and a big and chilly house in a strange neighbourhood, he regularly used to stop off at his parents' cottage, near his work, for a drink and a chat on the way home. There, with a deep-pile carpet beneath him and a bowlful of home-made cheese straws at his elbow, he would relate the triumphs and trials of his day to his Mum. She was an interested, intelligent, stimulating listener. As we will all be one day, when we can get some sleep and not be responsible for anyone's socks but our own. When he went home to a wife physically exhausted by the babies' bathtime and still staring hopelessly at the contents of the fridge, he could not help comparing the two homes and the two women. It was his father who eventually blew the whistle on him by remarking (with great vision for his generation) that perhaps Eileen might like some help with getting the children to bed. But it was too late by then. Eileen and the children went home to her own mother.

You have to accept that it is hard for mothers to give up custody, especially when their sons marry young. One moment it is a Mum's job to worry about whether he is eating, whether he should see a doctor about that cold, and whether he is truly happy at work. The next thing she knows she is the Bridegroom's Mother, handing over to some fluttery little madam who never made a bed properly in her life and probably buys packet stuffing. One experienced Groom's Mother – three sons down, one to go – tells me that the moment when you stand in church watching him wed is like walking for the last time around a house you have lived in, looking at the places where your furniture used to stand and wondering what the new owner will do. The difference, of course, is that when a human being is handed on, the first woman's furniture, as it were, stays put. If Mum trained him to throw his clothes on the floor and expect thick gravy on the dot of seven, he will remain programmed. And, unlike a previous owner, Mum will still be around, flitting through the rooms of his life to see how marriage has changed them. 'She's such a foodie, you know, won't let him ever have beans on toast,' moans Mother. Or, 'He used to be such a generous boy, but since he married Anita he keeps his cash in a purse.'

On the other hand, mothers do want their children to be happy. And one of the best ways of deflecting criticism, interference and general mischief-making is to be happy: visibly, lightheartedly, flippantly happy. Men! (and women, if it happens that way round) Hearken to this advice! If the marriage has problems, your mother is not the person to consult until things really couldn't be worse: she may be fatally disposed to take your side, even to the point of hindering reconciliation or reform of the marriage. And if she doesn't take your side, you will be outraged, and that won't help either.

Fathers-in-law

. . . rarely cause any trouble to their daughters-in-law, since if they dislike them they generally, and most sensibly, take the option of avoiding them entirely and wandering off into the garden. Or down to the pub with their sons. But the relations between fathers of girls and their sons-in-law can get not unlike the mothers-and-daughters-in-law problem. Except that mothers-in-law have plenty of domestic and child care ammunition to throw, and by tradition all a man can accuse his son-in-law of is not being a good provider. And it is money which tends to spark off masculine family disputes. If you want a cautionary tale, try Simon's.

His wife Susie has a powerful and wealthy father who dotes on her. Every time she incautiously mentions that they are saving up for something – a microwave oven, perhaps, or a dishwasher, or a holiday – he ups and pays for it, or has it delivered to them the next day. Susie cannot see any problem with this. Simon can. It makes him feel small. He mentioned this once to his father-in-law, who thought he was crazy. 'Can't I buy a present for my own little girl?' he said. 'Anyway, you can't expect to do everything for her any more, that's what the feminists say, isn't it? She earns her own money, and I give her the odd present.' Simon is still not happy. Especially when the presents are for their child, who is now getting old enough to know that she can get anything off Grandad.

Of course there are other ways to get on the wrong side of your father-in-law. You can sponge off him; borrow his car and crash it; or cheat on his darling daughter. Or send his darling grandson to the wrong sort of school. On the whole, though, straw-polling and reports from all social classes suggest that men are far more likely to go down to the pub happily with their fathers-in-law, rejoicing together at not having to peel the potatoes or listen to people talking about afterbirths. Either that, or ignore each other entirely.

Grannies

When the first baby appears, suddenly mothers-in-law become different creatures entirely. They want to be useful. They fear being excluded. This often makes difficult ones nicer, and nice ones difficult. Nell Dunn, who wrote a wonderful book of interviews with grandmothers, said that at the moment of her own first grandmotherhood she told herself, 'Don't expect to be happy, just get on with being useful. But I felt quite lost. I wasn't the mother of the child. I had to get used to being just a grandmother, and not the little princess in the bed with the newborn little prince, as I had been when his father was born. Instead there I was, with sleeves rolled up, being useful.' A grandmother, she acutely observes, is much lower down in the power scale than her own son or daughter, and it can be a shock. 'There is a sadness about it. You are further from the centre of life and nearer to death.'

But given any weakness or incompetence in the new mother, natural bossiness reasserts itself, in both mothers and mothers-in-law. They smell fear, grannies do. If the couple present a united, confident front and make it very clear that they have worked out their own priorities in child care and family-building, and welcome help but not interference, most families settle into an individual *modus vivendi* between the generations.

Very individual. As usual in family life, there is no point looking sideways with envy at other set-ups: some couples have marvellous, energetic, constantly babysitting grandmothers; some have busy old Woopies who enjoy their retirement far too much to be bothered with crumbs and tantrums and potties, and are forever jetting off on Saga holidays. Some have older, or prematurely old and shaky, grandparents who are themselves as much of a practical worry as the children. But every

sort has its advantages: jet-setting grannies can bring odd presents and tales of distant places, and the old and shaky ones can sit, and listen, and tell stories of long ago. You have to start from where you are, and make the best use of the raw material you have. Don't look sideways.

Aunts and Uncles and Honoraries

Whether genuine blood relations or honorary title-holders, aunties and uncles are extremely good news in any family. Only-children, on giving birth, should recruit as many godparents and close family friends as they can to be pseudo-unks in the family. Cousins, of course, are always nice (if only as a salutary lesson to your own children that there are some people in this world you damn well have to be nice to, whether you like it or not). But feckless, fancy-free bachelor uncles and aunts are particularly valuable. Remember that children's view of the world is very closely bounded by their social circle: if you live in 'couple country', forever mixing with other couples (or harassed single parents), and they have no brothers or sisters out in the world, children have no way of knowing that there is any other way to live than as a busy, scrambling, domestically obsessed parent of young children. Have they? And you don't want them to think that growing up has got no more to offer than ending up like you, do you?

So the presence of a snoring hungover uncle on the sofa, an elderly Bohemian friend playing the violin rather badly in the back bedroom or a tarty auntie spraying herself with Fracas in the bathroom, is – even if slightly fraying to the temper of whoever is expecting them at the lunch-table – in fact a huge contribution to family life. You can get wonderful friendships springing up between children of all ages and single people: childless people have few preconceptions about the new generation, and are generally intrigued and charmed that these creatures actually speak. Your infuriating teenager may seem quite reasonable to them: they too quite like sleeping till noon and dancing till three. It is you, even if you are twenty years younger than the bachelor uncle or auntie, who are ex-officio tedious old wrinklies, obsessed with rules. Also, not having children of their own to boast to, your single friends will be full of interesting stories about how they once knew a man who rode the wall of death with a lion cub on his shoulders, or how they nearly got run over by a rhinoceros on their wildly expensive safari holiday.

The home lives of these bachelor uncles and aunties is also fascinating to nicely brought up children. We have a cherished friend, a sculptor in his late fifties, who lives in splendid eccentricity, in a house full of works of art and bits of things which might one day be works of art. But what my children love best is to see him whisk open a kitchen drawer to reveal onion-peelings, apple cores, potato skins and every kind of vegetable detritus lying there mixed up. 'The soup drawer,' he explains tranquilly. 'Next week's food.' Another niece, writing once about her single aunt, said reverently that the best thing about her was that 'we go to snazzy restaurants and we can keep running around because she gives us money to feed the parking meter against the law, and lets us keep some of it too'. Other bachelor uncles and aunts and godparents may offer, as years go by, recherché sports, peculiar outings, shocking political ideas and – most of all – an audience willing to listen to a teenager's disgraceful ideas and plans for a university-free future. Or for life with a horrifically undesirable boyfriend.

These spare adults are vital: they represent the adult world, but an impartial adult world which has not invested emotional energy in you, and therefore is willing to watch you make your own mistakes. They are wonderful confidantes: if I had not had my aunt Dorothy at some stages of my teens, life would have been a lot bleaker.

And with a bit of luck, if you have played your cards right, the aunt or uncle will confide right back in you, and give you some pretty good advice. Especially about the horrific boyfriends and girlfriends. One I know always advises the parents that the only way to get rid of a dreadful suitor is to welcome him or her with open arms, keep saying 'How lovely to see you, Killer! Do tell me what the gang's been up to this week!' or 'Amanda! You must tell me where you got that skirt! I wish I had the figure for neoprene!' Your children will drop them like a hot brick if you do this, apparently.

Squeaky wheels and hereditary pests

One of the great unsung advantages of contact with the extended family and with outsiders is that it makes life much easier for misfits. You know what I mean: misfit children, squeaky wheels, black sheep, the ones you sigh over. Every large family has one, and in the days when large families were common, everyone knew that fact of life and accepted it. 'Oh, it's just Adrian, never mind him, you know what he's like.' If the family was really lucky, its members took turns to be the difficult one, with each younger member emerging from a Bad Phase just in time for the next one to go into it. There might even be a brief lull, during which Dad or Mum could afford to run off the rails a bit themselves. But as often as not, the same squeaky wheel went on squeaking, and everyone else went on putting up with it. 'Ah well, she's never been easy, from a baby. I'm sure she'll start speaking to us again/bring back the family silver/leave the Moonies. When she's done a bit of growing up.'

The trouble is today that, with so many tidy little two-child families, we have lost the knack of accommodating the less sociable and more chippy members. You have your two children and stop; and especially if they are a pigeon-pair, boy and girl, everyone says, 'Aaaah! You've got your little family now!' and expects you to be marvellously symmetrical, united and tidy and loving and generally similar.

Life, however, is not like that. Whether you have ten children or two, the possibility of one turning out to be a really difficult personality – not disturbed, you understand, not abused or unloved or furnished with any particular excuse, but nonetheless bloody difficult – remains. It is one of the reasons I hesitated long and hard before writing this book: it is fatally easy, in offering advice and sympathy about family life, to give the impression that if you had done everything correctly and wisely from the start, if you had been relaxed enough, loving enough, well organized enough – then all the family would be model citizens and get on well together.

Which is rubbish. Babies are born with quite a lot of their personalities already in position. We can certainly, by extreme cruelty or neglect, warp them into being suspicious and sad and unloving and eventually delinquent; but we cannot conversely guarantee that they will be easy to get on with. Some perfectly good, well-brought-up, basically sound people I know are incredibly difficult to be with: vague, or eccentric, or inordinately self-centred, or distant to the point of rudeness, or so clever in one direction – like computers, or creative writing – that they are almost imbecile in others. Bad parents are certainly responsible for some bad behaviour, but not for all of it. You may do everything right – insofar as there is a 'right' way to do it – and still end up with a squeaky wheel in the family.

The reason extended families help in coping with these oddballs is that being an oddball might actually be hereditary. Some women report the unnerving experience of lying on the delivery table, awash with emotion, only to find their husband's appalling Uncle Reggie staring up at them from the depths of a white cellular blanket. A smaller Uncle Reggie, perhaps, but unmistakably him: the eyes, the nose, the mouth turned down with a slight, knowing leer. For a moment, they gasp. Then the little pink mouth opens and bawls, and everything falls back into place: this is not Uncle Reggie. It is not even a boy. It is your new baby girl and you love her. And with luck, the resemblance to Uncle Reggie will pass.

One of the most fascinating things about new babies is the way that family likenesses keep flitting across their little faces. The genetic kaleidoscope has been shaken, two tribes have united, and for the first days, with some babies, you find yourself spotting a second-cousin here, an ancestor there, a grandparent's grimace there; a half-forgotten aunt from childhood

reappearing for a moment, a lost parent reborn in an early smile. The baby is, however, an individual. Different. Unique. But at the same time it has got Mummy's big eyes and Daddy's temper, and Granny's sense of humour and –

Yes, quite probably. Uncle Reggie's wild and antisocial streak, too. A little souvenir of the black sheep of the last generation. If you come of a happy tribe, this will simply be part of the fun. It will be delightful to brush your little boy's hair back one day and suddenly rediscover your own favourite brother's features at the age of five. If you are proud of your artist sister or your husband's cousin being a soloist in the Berlin Philharmonic, you will be happy to meet these gifts again in your scribbling and drum-banging children. It is especially useful to have a friendly extended family when you have a child who is nothing like either of you in character. Suppose you are both home-loving and steady, and the child longs only for adventure: the odds are that as she or he grows up, somewhere among the grandparents or uncles or cousins there will be a person who understands. Perhaps one who has actually been and had the adventures.

Suppose you are wildly sociable, and he is shy and bookish: you may try to be sympathetic, but there may be someone in the family who can go one better, and actually empathize, understanding from the depths of their own self what he wants and how he feels. At large family gatherings you sometimes see cousins, of widely different ages, who rarely meet, recognizing one another almost with a start of joy: I am not like my parents, I am not like my brother – but I am like you, they think. Not alone.

But this is if you are a happy tribe. What do you do if your child reminds you of a mortal enemy? It is not an idle question: one woman I know was happy with her first daughter, but when her second was born saw with horror that the baby looked very like her grandmother, the husband's mother, a cold and maliciously bitter woman who had done her best to break up their courtship, refused to attend the wedding, and disowned her son for marrying outside his class. Already exhausted, she was plunged into a postnatal depression which took months to clear. She found it hard not to shake the baby fiercely when she looked at her pursing her lips with just that refined expression, just that sour mouth, from which she had suffered so much in the past. The baby's appearance changed, but the mother was chastened for ages. 'I could have hated her. Even now I sometimes catch a gesture that is old Celia's, and I gulp.'

Some children bring down unwarranted wrath on their heads for small offences, merely because of a chance physical resemblance or an old memory which has nothing to do with them. For instance, if you were a single father and your wife a vain and selfish woman who dumped her daughter at birth and ran off with a man who said he could get her a modelling contract – well, you are not going to be too thrilled when your little girl starts staring into the mirror and saying 'pwetty me', are you? Or if your own father was a drunkard who wrecked his family, you might overreact rather sharply to your teenage son's first adventure with a bottle of cider.

You have to recognize this, and laugh it off, and not allow any child to become the official Black Sheep merely because of family legend. The nature/nurture debate swings to and fro in every generation: forty years ago nature ruled, and the families of convicted murderers often changed their names so that the children should not be stigmatized, while women adopting orphans were given awful warnings by their friends that 'you don't know the heredity . . .' Today the pendulum has swung right in the other direction, and it is fashionable to blame upbringing (mothers, usually) for every beer-can hurled off the terraces and stolen car driven into a jewellers' shop. No doubt there is something to be said on both sides: every parent knows perfectly well that their child has had certain characteristics from birth which are shared with their progenitors, and certain quite baffling ones. All you can do is tone down the antisocial ones and encourage the better impulses.

Because the kaleidoscope does shake out a new pattern every time, from the garish chips off various old blocks. As you lie on that delivery table, staring in horror at Uncle Reggie's leer, you can take heart. Perhaps all that misdirected energy, that devious cunning and shallow charm which led Reggie into a career of fraud, larceny, and conning rich widows will merely turn your daughter into something relatively harmless and acceptable. A journalist, perhaps?

11: Schooldays (and the Nights Between)

I wrote before (in *How Not to Raise a Perfect Child*) about managing the period when a child first starts school. Many of the same principles continue to matter in later school life: i.e. don't send your child to a school if the head teacher gives you the creeps, look for the buzz and hum of real interest rather than any chilly statistic off a league table; keep in touch with teachers, and if you can possibly make the time, involve yourself up to the neck in PTAs, governorships, classroom helping, fetes and plays and the rest. Bring school friends as firmly into home life as you can. In other words, don't let school be an alien place to which your children go: let it become an extension of their circle of family and friends. That way, apart from anything else, you will have a better idea of what is going on, and what influences are in your child's life.

But as the years go by, for heaven's sake cool it. If there is one thing worse than a completely uninterested primary school parent who hardly knows what the school is called, it is the parent of a teenager who won't back off. I feel particularly strongly about over-interfering parents because I can already feel the symptoms coming on, in myself. Several times already – with pre-teen children – I have been forcibly reminded by them that they are not babies and will sort out various problems or tackle difficulties with teachers by themselves. They are telling me about the problem with the rugby team, or the unfair punishment, because they want a sounding-board. Not an avenging Fury. If I keep sticking my oar in too obviously, they will stop telling me the problems. So I sit on my hands, and bite my tongue. It is their life. I chose the school, but I can't be at it. Even when asked to accompany a class trip to a museum (Oh yes! Yes! anything rather than work! I love coaches, and museums, and gossiping with teachers, I do!) I humbly ask my son whether he minds my intruding on his other world. So far, he doesn't. But the time will come when it is my turn to fade into the wallpaper . .

A few parental actions, however, do help with schooldays.

Listen. If there is one thing that parents of growing-up children all agree on, it is that the job is even trickier than having toddlers or primary school children. Young children are often very ready, bursting indeed, to tell you about their day. So if you are around, for a reasonable number of days in the week, straight after school you will get the full story. As they get older they wait, and brood, and choose their moment to come out with something devastating ('I think Mr Farthingale fancies me, he looks at me in a funny way in Biology class' – or 'Mum, do purple pills with yellow bits on count as drugs?') And even if this moment is half-way through your favourite programme or at eleven o'clock at night, it would be rash not to listen.

Try to understand the school's ethos. A school is not an efficient information filling-station: it has a strong pastoral, moral influence on your child, or else it is not much of a school. But its ideals may not be quite the same as yours, and there can be odd clashes. I remember bristling at a Speech Day when the guest, an old ex-Lord-Lieutenant, kept telling the children that 'the most important thing is a stable society – remember that, children, a stable society', as if Ceaucescu's Romania hadn't been stable. And Brezhnev's Russia. Luckily, I knew that the head teacher had pretty strong views about a free society, and a loving society, and a fair one too, and was probably cringing through the speech as much as I was. If I had not known this, I might have grown a bit hostile at this point.

Another mother told me of her shocked surprise when she realized that the sex education the school was giving her daughter was exclusively about health and the avoidance of AIDS and other diseases: but anybody else who had had a child pass through that school could have told her that if she wanted any mention of marriage, love, fidelity or procreation, she had signed on at the wrong window. It was famous for its secular, pragmatic, OK-if-you-use-a-condom philosophy. I am not saying that you have to agree with everything the school teaches in the line of 'PSME' – the jargon for personal, social and moral education – but if you know its line, you can discuss such matters with your children yourself, challenge the school view, and generally broaden their outlook without coming over all outraged. It does no harm to point out to older children that being a whizz at Maths does not necessarily make a teacher sound on the subject of sex. Or religion. Or race relations.

Keep the rules. The uniform may seem to you to be outdated, impractical, and even a touch perverse (Why the hell must little boys wear shorts in mid-winter at certain schools? What is this curious fetish about quenching glowing, growing girls in grey polyester pleats?) but if you have committed yourself to a school for other reasons, you are stuck with it. Also with other things which may annoy you, as a sane person (such as Saturday morning school, or funny rules about length of hair and skirts). You can protest mildly, but there is no point in encouraging your child to break rules, however silly they seem. You can say that you agree they are silly, of course; point out that in adult society we all spend half our time obeying damn silly rules, like not parking on double yellow lines in deserted market towns, and that we do it for the sake of general law and order and the Greater Good of all. Perhaps you could point out that Mummy's office doesn't allow trousers. Or that Daddy has to wear a tie every day of his working life. Tell them that if they work hard and pass their exams, they might grow up to be the people who change the silly rules.

Do not get educationally neurotic. Difficult, this one, in an era of recession and educational reform, when every saloon-bar philosopher has a theory about what is wrong with our schools, and opportunist educational psychologists are forever touting for business and setting up reading-and-maths-age tests you can do by post to check up on your child. There is a very fine line between noticing that a child is not learning much, and getting obsessively pushy about it. In education, there will always be parents who don't care, parents who do, and parents who care far too much.

I once, for journalistic reasons, imposed one of the correspondence tests on my own daughter (chosen because she actually enjoys exams very much). She sat down to the paper and with many a modish cry of 'Aye carumba!' and 'Eat my shorts!' batted through it in half an hour, reading from 'jam' to 'incandescent', though unaccountably failing to spell 'champagne'. Shows you the sort of household she comes from. Lots of jam, and no champagne. The psychologist diagnosed her reading and maths ages, rather impressively, much as her school had done, but then shocked me by saying, 'She's a super reader, good speller, and fine on maths, but not as high. That's where she should concentrate.' At this point a philosophical difference emerged between us: why should the poor child concentrate on maths when she was well up to the average? 'Because in order to fulfil her potential,' said the psychologist sternly, 'a bright child should be ahead in every area.' We never agreed. It seemed to me that you should be allowed to be an Einstein in maths with-

out being forced to read books above your age group. Or an adventurous and accomplished reader who just struggled along normally in maths, or an obsessive natural-historian who knew all about the life cycle of slugs, but showed little promise of distinction elsewhere. Every child needs balance, and to accomplish the basic normal standards: but being good at one thing should not lay upon you a burden to be good at everything.

Don't press the school to accelerate a bright child. This is a controversial thing to say. A lot of parents feel a bright child is bored among its age group, and are all for pushing him or her up two or three years. This happened to me – not because I was bright, but because I came from an advanced educational system, in France, to a backward one in Johannesburg for a year. When I was twelve, I was in a class of heavily pubescent fifteen-year-olds. I have to tell you it was not a success. If a child really is too bright for their class, a freer approach to personal study could be urged on the school: many will accommodate it. It is occasionally true that a child is mature enough to mix with others two years older on a regular basis. But most of them can't, and hate it. A girl I knew came up to University at fifteen and a half instead of eighteen, and much good it did her: out of her depth for three years socially, she eventually turned against her own gifts, married at nineteen and has hardly looked at a book since.

Changing school

It is a truism that changing schools is stressful for a child. One or two even run away at this time, or develop mysterious illnesses. They need as much support from their home base as anyone else undergoing a rite of passage: a bride, an exile, a newly and dizzily promoted executive. They are even, in a sense, bereaved: children who leave a good primary school are losing a close and familiar family of teachers, even if they stay among their friends. And often they leave their friends as well, to go into a whole new culture, with different slang, different habits, and higher expectations.

Matters are not helped if the parents, too, are feeling bereaved. A good primary school – the first outside body to which you ever entrust your child – can creep into your family life as a very important influence. If you are active, help with parties and outings, sit on the PTA or act as a classroom volunteer, your life too will be changed when your child leaves (our primary school was so wonderful that a lot of parents couldn't bear to leave the PTA, and stayed on it for ridiculous lengths of time while their children were at secondary school). A psychiatrist once told me that she sees a lot of mothers, in particular, whose children have just gone to secondary school, and who find themselves plunged into unaccountable depression. If the new school is a bus or train run away, and you no longer have a daily meeting at the school gate with the other parents, you may feel even more bereft. And if – as bigger schools often do – it keeps parents at a cooler distance than your friendly little first school, you may get positively upset. Moreover, if there has been conflict between parents as to which school the child should go to, even more tension is generated.

I am not saying all this will happen to you. But watch out for it. Children pick up the moods and doubts of their parents very easily: they need to go to the new school with optimism and confidence. It deserves a fair trial, and they deserve to go there in hope, not fear. If the parent is tearful and fearful, it might be best if that parent kept clear of the first school runs, leaving it to the other, calmer one (there you are, yet another hurdle for single parents. Sorry. Is there perhaps an uncle, or aunt, who might help restore your perspective?).

Conversely, of course, if you have fought hard or made financial sacrifices to get your child into the particular school of your dreams, you want to avoid giving the impression that you value the school more than the child. If he or she absolutely hates it, at least listen to that point of view. If the child goes on hating it for a long time, consider giving up your dream and moving him or her. It may have fabulous science labs, elegant grounds and a superb academic reputation – and still be a rotten depressing hole. I remember once congratulating a new acquaintance who mentioned that her children were at a school which had topped a league in one of the proliferating 'Good Schools Guides'. She snapped: 'I'm moving them next term. It's an appalling place. They pass all their exams, but they've never had a school outing or a school play, the teachers never seem to crack a smile, the children are exhausted and nervous, and the headmaster is a raging racist snob whose assemblies are somewhere to the right of a Nuremberg rally.'

Her children are now perfectly happy – and learning well enough, and more willingly – at a school which never got within a mile of any league table.

12: A Woman's Work

Every now and again some rash headmistress invites me to Speech Day. 'Tell the girls how a woman can combine a career and a family,' she suggests. So I do.

'The secret, girls,' I begin, 'is never, ever to do any housework. And moreover, spend no time whatsoever on your personal appearance. That way you release hours of time for work and playing with children.' At which point I feel the gimlet eye of the home economics teacher sizing up my safety-pinned hem and Ken Dodd hairstyle, and hear the strangled gasps of a matron who has spent four years trying to instil the notion of 'grooming' into her gels, and it is time to shin off down the fire escape before they get to me.

But the fact is that whoever carries it out – Mum, Dad, Nanny, Granny – mothering a family is a job. And someone has to do it. And if it is done in addition to an earning job, something will have to give. Houseproud fidgeting and eyebrow-plucking are, to me, the obvious candidates to be flung out of the balloon-basket of life. You may have other ideas.

But remember also that paid work needs to be considered as part of the family picture. All this happy creative affectionate home life has got to be paid for, somehow. Unless you have no choice but to live on meagre State benefits, at least one of you is going to need to work. Probably, for some of the time anyway, two of you: our generation in the West has painted itself into a corner so effectively with absurd housing costs, consumer goods seen as essentials and a spiral of personal credit, that for a great many families there is no option but for both parents to earn. If they get a chance.

And besides, work is satisfying. It links you in to the outside world, gives you a place beyond the family circle and a useful wider perspective. You can return to a cross, fed-up child who temporarily hates school with more real understanding if you have spent your own day getting fed up with your colleagues and boss. Besides, working parents are a constant reminder to a child or teenager that the virtues of punctuality, conscientiousness, and turning up to work even when you don't feel like it are not tiresome abstract disciplines or futile things urged on schoolchildren to torment them. They are the way adult human beings get to earn their daily bread, and put jam on it.

Whether a mother works while her children are young is up to her, and to circumstance. As I wrote in my first book, being guilty about it is a waste of time. If you feel guilty, don't work. If you have no choice but to work – either because the family needs the money or because you get seriously depressed staying at home full-time – then don't feel guilty. Come home smiling, and as early as humanly possible; and make the weekends really good for everyone. Even if it means skimping the housework and cooking (and it does, it does). And don't patronize or criticize your sisters who don't work outside the home for being 'housewives': different systems suit different people, and all children are different in their susceptibilities and how happy they can be with nurseries or nannies. There are happy families in both camps, and bloody miserable ones too.

But one word of warning: it is absolutely essential to talk out any conflict between fathers and mothers about dual careers. A working mother can be undermined, fatally, by the spoken or unspoken criticism of her husband. So can a stay-at-home mother. Good humour, kindness, and mutual support are essential in both cases: if you really can't agree, then debate it.

As children get older, the problem changes. They make their own breakfast, may pack their own sandwiches; they are at school until quite late, they can travel home alone and come in with latch-keys, and they have decided views of their own about what to do in the holidays. But they still need you, and in some ways it is harder to fit in their needs: because the older a child gets, the more unpredictable are the moments when he or she wants to talk things over. Like at eleven o'clock at night. And you still have to be there, to be talked at. Sometimes the mothers who behave most callously in their children's teens are not those who went back to work when their children were tiny; having always felt a bit uneasy about leaving the children, they continue to come home from the office wanting to work on their relationship, well into the teen years. I have met several mothers who stayed at home faithfully until their children were eight or nine, and then took up a career again with an ambitious passion which almost wiped out their family life. The subtext here was, 'Look, I gave you a decade of my life. Now push off and leave me alone.' The children didn't think much of that.

The great challenge for a woman – and also for a man, because men are starting to get the message – is to balance that ambitious working passion with the emotional needs of family life. It is not an impossible balance to find, but it is a tricky one. There has been a post-feminist backlash recently against that monster of myth, the hard-eyed, shoulder-padded 'Career Mum'. Dewy-eyed films and novels have appeared, starring women who (like Diane Keaton in *Baby Boom* or the batty TV executive in Maeve Haran's *Having It All*) decide to leave the bitter, combative boardroom world to stay at home with their babies, and then set up cosy little Aga-centred businesses at home which threaten to become huge and drag them back into the Stock Market. What irritates me about all this is the posing: the all-or-nothing approach which suggests that a woman is either a hard bitch in smart suits, with a briefcase, or a lovely Mummy in soft heathery cardigans who arranges dried flowers. There is never any suggestion that it is possible to make both corporate decisions and apple pies; no space for women who run businesses but have crooked hems, or dare to own both Agas and briefcases.

Doing justice to children and a career is not easy; but then, nor is it easy to mix a job with a passion for local politics, or ocean-racing, as men have done for ages. Adult mothers apply the same intelligence to their life as to their job. Any fool can see that small children will not thrive if they never know when they will see their mother again; any fool can see the drawbacks of trying to combine parenthood with jobs without boundaries:

the kind which suck you in, hype you up, and render you unfit for any but colleagues' company. One of the most nauseating complaints of the age is that the high-flying career woman is somehow 'a victim': she does not have to be. Trapped, underpaid workers must suffer silently as they struggle home by public transport to the childminder; executive women, and men, can use their money and clout to reorganize the schedule and hurry home.

And they do, in real life. A BBC news producer tells the story of meeting Harriet Harman, MP, on the train away from the Labour conference at Brighton the day before the big speeches. It turned out that both women were dashing home – Ms Harman for a school function, the producer to treat her three children with headlouse shampoo. They were both back by dawn. Another woman, a senior manager in a large company, celebrated her pregnancy by going to the MD with the information that she had done an analysis of the department's work, and that he had three-quarters of a job vacancy, just below her level. She offered to swap her full-time job for it, three-and-a-half days a week. He agreed. The undramatic truth is that women who value their family life often make the decision to give up time, money, and status; but not necessarily all of it.

Ways off the treadmill: working at home

When employers are inflexible, some women (and a few child-caring men) go ingeniously independent. During the peak years of the Thatcher Government, cocktail guests at No. 10 Downing Street were often fed by a small, determined catering firm consisting of two women from Suffolk with seven children under ten between them. In the cartoon universe of female stereotypes, this would have blown up into a million-pound business, with its directors wearing power blouses and neglecting their children and husbands. As it is, they continued to turn up at the school gates looking faintly dishevelled, but triumphant, even after their biggest functions.

A lot of us take the option of working at home. Or, as we like to say, 'from home', which gives the impression that we get out of the damn place more often than we do. Sales reps can do this (a good few men do, successfully, and mind their children for part-time working wives as well). Journalists can do it, so can teleworkers in companies like F International, most of whose staff are outworkers; so do illustrators, copy editors, dress-makers, knitters, craftspeople and caterers.

It can be terrific. Instead of travelling to work, you shamble into the spare bedroom, or the kitchen, possibly still in your dressing-gown, and there you are. At work. If children are home sick from school, you can let them read, or lie around in your work room, grumbling softly and being chucked the occasional sandwich. Even the smallest children can be trained not to pick up the telephone when it rings, and not to interrupt you while you are on it. Even the most inconsiderate teenager can be persuaded that if he steals all your paper and envelopes, your wrath will be so great it isn't worth it. You soon learn such basic skills as conducting a professional conversation with a sharp-clawed kitten climbing up your trousers, ignoring the mound of washing-up until evening, putting up shelves which don't crash down on your computer, and recognizing the distinctive footsteps of a Jehovah's witness or a time-wasting neighbour on the front path in time to dive under the desk. Your full-time-housewife friends and assorted relations also get into the habit of asking whether it is a good moment to ring/call/deliver the parish newsletter/flop at your kitchen table with the gory details of their operation. Working at home saves money, and fossil fuel, and is generally a green and sensible way to operate.

But beware. I have been a homeworker for eleven years, and many is the morning when I would give anything to go to a chummy office instead of a chilly, messy, lonely little room. I yearn for a cup of canteen coffee and an update on the temp's love-life – but what I get is a blank screen and a telephone. I look forward keenly to ten minutes' company at the school gates every afternoon, and the worst day of my life was when we got our own fax machine: I used to go to the Post Office and have a little chat and it was the highlight of my day.

Down the ages, writers have complained about the loneliness of their craft; telecommuting will extend that isolation to other workers. Nobody prone to loneliness, no newly separated woman with her children growing independent, should attempt it. There are times when we need an office the way that debs need dances. The absence of a visible, fussing boss may seem like a bonus (and indeed, on a sunny spring morning it is a great privilege to go for a bike ride or a swim, knowing you can make up the time overnight). But a homeworker needs to be her or his own fussy boss: you require iron discipline, what with the biscuits and the coffee and the children's computer-games

so close at hand. Many people frankly fall apart. They straighten paper clips, they make tea, they read the old newspapers in the cat-litter tray and decide to turn out the kitchen drawers.

If both partners work at home, they may discover that their marriage actually thrived on separations and reunions and gossip from the outside world. Young mothers can go weepy and depressed when they look out of the study window and see an au pair playing in the sun with their baby while they are trying to revise the sales figures. And some of us are fatally untidy. My study, without the discipline of a fierce secretary or ruthless office-cleaner, is a nightmare of torn-up paper, scribbled notes, tottering bookshelves, unanswered letters and obsolete tangles of cable. I dress like a tramp. If I were a factory, the council would close me down. Consider your strengths and weaknesses before you take the plunge.

Part-time work and jobshares

Logistically these are the ideal solution for working mothers. But ambitious, talented women ought to consider, however briefly, the emotional implications. In many professions, part-time work attracts not much respect, and nor do jobshares. If you really are a high-flyer, undamped by maternal hormones, a little work can feel worse than none: you have perforce to take instructions from people less talented, but without your home responsibilities. You can get frustrated and morose. At worst, you might take it out on the children, and even if this only happens in your secret thoughts it is a very depressing thing to do. I used to have a colleague who would smash up breadsticks savagely in Fleet Street restaurants and tell anyone who would listen that 'If it hadn't been for the blasted, blasted children I would have been an editor by now . . .' This is not constructive. If you are going to compromise because your family is of high value to you, and at a phase which needs you, then recognize that you are doing it, and weigh the demands of what you see as duty against those of personal fulfilment. Get it all out in the open. And be prepared to modify your decision, in either direction, if it clearly isn't working.

Dual careers

If a married couple both work, and intend to go on living together, there has to be some kind of agreement on whose career matters most at any given moment. The crunch point may be a big one – like relocation to the other side of Europe – or it may be a small one, like who is going to be late for work in order to go home and fetch the cello your son forgot to take in on orchestra day. Women are better at sidelining the importance of their careers (though they sometimes grow bitter, later on). Most men find it very painful and embarrassing to play second fiddle to a wife. That does not mean that they should never do so; but the wife concerned should exercise a certain tact and chivalry about the matter. And it goes without saying that if her own high-flying career has disrupted the family and called for sacrifices of time and convenience from her husband, she automatically forfeits all right to suggest – ever – that her husband is not pulling his financial weight. Family men are rarely allowed, these days, to be autocratic because they are breadwinners. Women shouldn't try it on, either.

I refer you to the case of my former friend Jeanette (not her real name). She is an actress, whose accountant husband refused promotions for years so that he could guarantee to be home with the three children while she did evenings and tours. She did very well, became well-known and well-off, but in latter, weird and menopausal, years forgot all about his support and railed at her husband instead for 'living off her work' and 'sponging'. She also told the children rather inaccurately that she had always 'had to work, to support the family'. He left her, and serve her right. Women can be as nasty as men when they try.

Working colleagues

One of the great advantages of women having invaded the workplace in greater numbers is that, at last, our sex is getting to understand the joys of relationships with colleagues. And is therefore being less mean and suspicious about our husbands' working friendships. There are real loves, hates, tendernesses and comradeships in office life – and real betrayals, too. People do not stop being human just because they are at work. You can't shut them away from nine to five and expect them not to have emotions during that time. So even the most cool and professional people will develop friendships at work – even if they don't see those people outside.

What both partners in a family have to understand is that this does not necessarily mean an affair. A man who gets home and begins every sentence with 'Lucinda says –', or a woman who becomes devoted to a male ally at work, and shares private jokes with him, is not necessarily on the point of wrecking the home. I once talked to such a pair of friends, neither of whose partners liked it one bit. Call them Vivien and James. They worked in the same television news department for five years. At first, he was the senior, then she rose to the same grade. Whenever they worked the same shift, an electric current flowed. Vivien called James 'a fabulous operator – as soon as he gets a hunch, he carries it through faster and with more flair than anyone I've ever seen. And he feels right, and reacts right, about everything. He's a good man, a man with a conscience, but a solid, tough news mind as well. He's a star, as far as I'm concerned. We could talk and argue over a drink all night, and not feel tired.'

James expressed the same mix of professional and personal praise. 'Viv just swishes into the office, no bullshit, gets right down to work – you should hear her on the phone, as tough as any man could be – but she's not one of those hard, crass birds who try to be Rambo. I've seen her cry about some terrible story, but never until the programme's over.'

Together, for five years, this pair had their wild, brilliant ideas, worked together like a well-oiled machine. And at the office party, a no-spouses function by long tradition, they danced like dervishes and hugged like children. And yes, you are there before me: Vivien's husband didn't like it one bit. He believed her when she reiterated that she was not physically unfaithful, but emotionally it was a moot point. Things cooled if James was mentioned at home. He – a divorced man well involved with another woman outside work – never envisaged an affair either. 'Never mind the morality, it would wreck the working relationship.' But his girlfriend grew jealous and tearful, and in the end he moved on to a new job and the friendship cooled off.

How do you handle this? If you are both out in the unisex working world, rather than him being penned safely in an all-male office and her at home by the hearth as would have probably been the case ninety years ago, these intense extra-marital friendships are bound to happen. Probably the best cure is to seize the bull by the horns, and move the friendship into the family where it is less threatening. Have Sunday lunches *à quatre*, with both sets of children if applicable. Mix partner and colleague, firmly. Rub their noses in it. Make both sides accept the other relationship. Don't give in, don't let your friendships with the rest of the human race be limited just because you have a family. Good luck . . .

Success, excuses, and cop-outs

One of the rarely discussed aspects of family life is how useful it is as an excuse. Anyone who has had children would probably confess to having used them as a cop-out. 'We'd love to come barn-dancing, but we can't get a babysitter . . . of course, we'd love to help, but with three children . . . well, we don't see enough of the dear old lady, but of course, you see, Justin gets carsick . . .' Sometimes the excuses are genuine, sometimes they are not. We take children's names in vain because we do not want to do things anyway. Mine stand round jeering in the kitchen when they hear me say soupily to some editor, 'Oh goodness, I'd love to do a feature about a lesbian folk-dancing group in Newcastle, but I'm a bit tied up, you see, with the children . . .' In the editorial office the childless women feel unable to argue, while fellow mothers and New Men nod sympathetically and think, 'What a saint that girl is!' And I wipe my brow and thank goodness that they do not know that I am about to skive off on my own for five days to Scotland, and that the children don't mind a bit because they will be able to get their father to take them to the chip shop more, and that the real reason I say no is that their proposal is a seriously bum idea.

This is all quite harmless, and using children as excuses serves to reinforce the perfectly healthy world-view that personal relationships are more important than notches on one's Filofax. But the child-as-excuse becomes more insidious when we begin to say, 'Look, I'm a working mother, I don't have time to dress up like a supermodel.' (Translation: I don't fit into the clothes any more.) Or 'Since the children, I simply can't keep up with the newspapers.' (Translation: I only read the features pages because thinking about Bosnia gives me a headache.) This can lead on to another refinement: we all know women who would have been the world's greatest brain surgeon if it hadn't been for their noble dedication to 'the children'. In the late Sixties there was a rash of novels about a figure known as the Captive Graduate Wife. This was inevitably a brilliant girl with so little sense that she married young, started breeding, and only then twigged that someone was going to have to look after these children. Sometimes this can end in real bitterness, as witness the number of thin-lipped, railing middle-aged women genuinely convinced that they have wrecked their lives for their ungrateful offspring.

It will not do. Most human beings are not straightforward creatures who see what they want and go for it; otherwise we would all be Richard Branson. Most of us are a walking web of indecision, held back by laziness, self-doubt and fear of failing. If there is a handy way to convince ourselves that we are actually being held back by saintliness, it feels much better. But family dependence is – though precious – fairly brief in its most intense phase. If you really were going to be a world-class novelist, you would be writing that novel now. On the kitchen table. If you don't want to, fine. But don't blame the poor children. Or husband. Or wife. Though men don't do it so much: I have yet to read a failed politician's memoirs in which he blamed his lack of lustre and power on the fact that his daughter was doing O levels and the baby kept him awake at night.

Confidence

Unfortunately for women who left the workplace when their children were young and try, in their forties or fifties, to return, fear of failing is increased by the very fact of motherhood. Jill Freud, wife of the MP, now runs her own theatre company. But I remember her once telling me that when she first tried to plunge back into the professional theatre after five children, the worst bit was to face auditions and realize that for the first time in years, you were not particularly important to anyone in the room. After being the heart of the family, the indispensable mum, it is hard to go back into the ranks. Some don't. They plead that the grandchildren will be needing them, any day now.

The same effect can hit younger women, too. I am constantly amazed by the shiny, brittle, snappy confidence of professional young women I know without children. Although I have always been, even from home, a part of the working world, I still have far more lapses of professional confidence as a mother than I ever did as a childless woman. It has something to do with the great vulnerability of mothers: you feel, from the first time your baby stirs, a sense that you have given a hostage to fortune. You know that one disaster – losing that child – could devastate you. You imagine it, all through babyhood, childhood, early independence. There is a pit at your feet, always. Your emotions are more widely diffused across the world. You cry in news bulletins for the sadness of the world's children. And sometimes that sense of a pit can extend itself into your working life, so that you feel uneasy, hesitant, unable to 'go for it' in the gung-ho way you might have done before.

But you pull yourself together, grit your teeth, and do it all the same. Because on balance, you have gained more than you have lost: the ability to sing some new notes, and understand a little more of the marvellous strangeness of life, to love the human race a little more. And, with luck, to carry that gentler vision out into the working world, and change some of its ways.

13: Money Matters and Testing Times

Another daydream . . .

Every time the Chancellor of the Exchequer stands up to present his annual Budget, making everything sound so reasonable and well-balanced (even when it turns out differently), I indulge in a daydream. Suppose I were to present my own? At three o'clock I should rise to my feet amid respectful silence around the kitchen table, adjust my glasses, shuffle my notes and begin:

'The past fiscal year has been a mixed one for the economy. On the one hand, considerable savings have been made in the area of Scalextric by this government's firm initiative in buying only the basic set.' (*Cries of 'Shame!', 'Yah!'*) 'On the other hand, the consumption of chocolate biscuits has risen out of control and requires firm fiscal management.' (*Catcalls, booing.*)

'On the clothing front, a blow was sustained by the simultaneous outgrowing of no fewer than five almost new pairs of school shoes, plimsolls and football-boots owing to rapid foot inflation. But in fairness, this additional burden has been partly offset by younger members' willingness – nay, determination – to spend every weekend in the same tracksuit bottoms which end two inches above the ankle and are full of rips.' (*Cries of 'Eeyah, eeyah, yah!'*) 'The cat food situation is also under review (*Miaow!*) following the calculation that two years' worth of the present brand would buy a week in the Seychelles. We have resolved on downgrading from Luxury Kittentreat to Bargain Gristlechunks.' (*Uproar in the House. Cries of 'Order, order!'*) 'Furthermore, owing to severe losses, the supply of replacement Cub woggles and karate belts is to be privatized, and borne from Pocket Money rather than central funds. Pocket Money itself is frozen,' (*cries of 'Shame! Resign!' Uproar, breaking of crockery. Bravely and with dignity, the Chancellor continues,*) 'and we are demanding co-operation from all members regarding excessive electricity consumption on landing lights. Moreover, a ceiling has been put on Scotch, gin, and other beverages of 1.4 litres per fortnight –'

And so on, until I sit down amid thunderous applause at five o'clock, having once more saved the domestic economy from ruin. All dreams, of course. Like most families not in immediate trouble, we shall muddle along, buying on impulse, saving the odd 2p on a special offer and immediately squandering £4.99 on the strength of it. Reason has little to do with family spending. If we have had a tough week at work we feel entitled to spoil ourselves or our children (it comes to almost the same thing, when you are in a good family mood). If we sustain a rush of affection for our spouse, out comes the plastic card to prove it. When a tax bill comes in, we economize in a fit of panic by buying cheaper biscuits, the kind we all hate, which are eventually fed to the birds.

But a decent approach to family finance is, alas, vital to a decent family life. If you have a lot of money it is easier than if you are skint, but even the wealthiest families often fall out over money. It has an unfortunate way of becoming a symbol of other things which you don't talk about. Like sex. Or a particular child going through a crucifyingly annoying phase. Or grand-parental interference in your life.

Who runs the money?

Whether you deal in large sums or small, high living or survival, whatever money there is has to be managed. And a family being a merged, corporate entity, it has to be managed quite differently from a carefree single's private loot. Ailean Mills of the Dorland advertising agency in London once remarked that whenever you do marketing surveys of couples and ask the question 'Who handles the family finances?', the men will reply unhesitatingly 'I do'. When the researcher asks the wife, in a separate room, the identical question, she too replies 'Oh, I do'.

You could hardly get a better cautionary introduction to the whole minefield of financial aggravation, misunderstanding and plain comedy that lies ahead of every pair of idealistic newlyweds. Possibly the two partners mean something different by 'handle the finances'. Perhaps the man means that he fills out the annual tax return and that he was the one who originally made the appointment with the building society about the mortgage. Whereas the wife means that she gets landed with regularly checking, paying, and filing the bills. Or perhaps the husband is the one who fiddles around at the desk for hours, putting bills on spikes and calling his overdraft a 'cash flow shortfall', but the wife considers she 'handles the family finances' because she is the one who juggles the housekeeping from day to day and makes crucial executive decisions as to whether the children can have new trainers before the old ones are actually gaping at the toes.

Or perhaps the husband is right, and the family is run on old-fashioned lines whereby the wife never sees a bill or a bank statement, but is ceremonially handed the Housekeeping Money every week and applies humbly to him for more. Even such traditional men, however, can be the type to be attracted to large-scale finance and prefer to leave penny-pinching to the women. One wonderful story concerned a wife who said that her husband had spent three hours reassessing their finances on his new computer, surrounded by rapidly emptying cans of beer as he created spreadsheet after spreadsheet, pie-chart after pie-chart, finally to emerge triumphantly at bedtime to announce that he had balanced the books and 'identified the areas of pressure', so that all that was needed was a 'downward readjustment' of 9.27% on household spending and children's clothes. 'He seemed so genuinely pleased and proud of this idea,' she said sadly, 'that I hadn't the heart to hit him with the poker.' The father was clearly a victim of the disease which grips so many governments: the touching belief that if it looks right on paper, it is right.

But some accommodation between temperaments has to be reached. Now that the days of the pretty-little-featherhead who doesn't trouble her head about money are over, wives are educated, and equal, and have to take a partnership role. Practicality and pride, independence and co-operation have to live together. The phrases 'Mean swine!' and 'Extravagant cow!' have no place in harmonious family life. Organization is the key.

Early in marriage, it pays to have decided very firmly how you are going to arrange your bank accounts and bills. No billing and cooing, no sentimentality, none of that stuff about endowing each other with worldly goods: these things do not go with banking. Wise newlyweds compose themselves to gravity, stop making vague promises about giving each other the earth, and soberly consider the pitfalls of each system. They might decide on the business where both pay their earnings into a joint account, and draw it as necessary. It sounds wonderful: but in practice, the word 'necessary' needs a bit of expanding upon. And besides, it immediately makes it impossible for either lovebird to give the other one a present without the bank statement unromantically revealing the price to both partners (besides, it doesn't feel like a present if you have paid half of it yourself). For another thing, it can get very depressing for the wife when she stops working to look after the children, either for a short time or a long one. A lot of women end up feeling very guilty about every penny they take out of 'his' money for themselves, and despite working an unremitting eighteen-hour day with toddlers they hardly feel justified in buying a lipstick or a Mars bar because they aren't formally putting anything in. It is depressed feelings like this which lead to the Wages for Housework campaign: in a society which measures people by their earning power, having no 'salary' can be lowering.

Curiously, there is evidence that when women are the only earners in the household, after a while they start developing traditional male patterns of meanness. One wrote in the *Guardian* that she had turned into an old-fashioned, mean and domineering 'husband' of the worst sort since her man had been out of work, and grudged him his large appetite, his extravagance with toilet-paper and even – I love this bit – his political opinions because she had paid for the newspaper which enabled him to have opinions at all.

Sometimes husbands and lower- or non-earning wives get round the danger of feeling this way by reverting to the old system of 'housekeeping money', generous enough for a proportion of it to be tacitly accepted as the wife's mad money out of which she can guiltlessly buy herself treats, and him presents. Personally, I think housekeeping money of this kind should be index-linked and earnings-related, but I have been unable to find one single case of this actually happening. The physical handing over of money depresses some previously independent women, too: a standing order can be more dignified.

Then, of course, there is the other traditional, more working-class system in which the wage-earner gets home and hands over the whole lot to his wife (or, I suppose, her husband, though I know of no such cases). The wife then hands him the beer money, and manages the rest herself. This can be a surprisingly cheerful arrangement. One man – a doctor, in fact, and quite a senior one – once told me that he was so disastrously bad with money that when his second child was born he gave up completely, and had his whole salary paid straight into his wife's bank account. She then handed him some pocket money every morning, and everything worked perfectly. He saved out of his pocket money to buy her presents, just as the children did. They kept one credit card of his, locked away in his wife's drawer, so that if he was travelling to a conference or on holiday he would not be embarrassed. The children, both being girls, find it exquisitely funny that they often have more cash than Daddy. My only worry about Daddy is that if he is ever widowed or divorced, he will be in exactly the same position as those dear-little-featherhead wives who have never seen a bill: middle-aged yet as clueless as a teenager.

If both partners are earning, and both keep their own bank accounts, you have to decide who pays what. Does he pay the mortgage, rates, and fuel while she pays food and holidays? Who gets the car serviced, the cat neutered? And is it fair to ask one partner to see all his salary dribble away on deeply boring bills, while the wife gets the satisfaction of signing cheques for fun and games and smart new sofas? One wife said to me that her money was to 'put jam on the bread' and that it nearly killed her to write a £200 cheque for new guttering once. 'Who could enjoy paying for a gutter?' But haven't men a right to such delicate feelings? Remember poor old Rumpole, in *Rumpole of the Bailey*, seeing his hard-won court fees 'recklessly expended on pan-scourers and Vim'? Perhaps true equality means that women will have to get used to paying for roofing-felt and car insurance. Of course, you could choose to split every single bill down the middle, like fiercely independent cohabiting couples, but that way you end up with complicated and deeply unromantic sessions late at night working out whether the gas bill and the TV licence added up to roughly the same as the telephone bill and the bulk consignment of vacuum-cleaner bags. But life is too short, in my view, for such self-inflicted miseries.

On the whole, I favour the increasingly common system of a joint account which is fed, in varying proportions, by two private ones. The joint account pays the house bills and standing orders; the private accounts, however small, remain strictly private. Psychologically, the best thing about this system is that once you have paid your standing order into the joint account, it doesn't feel like your own money any more – it is gone, and that is that. So in a mysterious way, all the household bills become 'free'. In a rather less mysterious way, of course, the joint account invariably becomes overdrawn, but every scheme has its snags. As Katharine Whitehorn once observed, a great many joint-accounting systems result in the creation of a curious commodity, 'imaginary money'. Some of us keep spending it. But even if the joint account is problematical, at least each one's private account can mount up or run down, for richer for poorer, according to its owner's temperament. £12.72 of your very own to squander is worth a hundred in the joint account, any day. Everyone needs a holiday from pinching pennies.

Pester power

Whatever your income, someone is after it. And their great new weapon is your children: marketeers and advertisers are now aiming campaigns directly and deliberately at the 'pester power' of children – their ability to persuade the family to buy particular products. Not only for them, but even for the dog: TV commercials even for dog and cat food have started to aim lower in age, and well below the belt, in tactics. There was a seminar in 1993 in London called 'Family dynamics and the shopping experience', where an advertiser said, 'The power and influence of children can be harnessed by manufacturers and retailers alike,' and met with thunderous applause. Another said, 'Children are extremely important as persuaders, and can't be ignored.'

Should you resist pester power in household shopping? Or is it a good idea – in the interests of family democracy and the development of your children's sense of responsibility – to let them have a say in what you buy?

My own view is that if you are going to give them that say, they have to work for it. Make them cost out the different cereals, work out the difference, decide whether the extra 70p for Oat 'n' Honey is worth it, how much difference it would make over the year, and what else you might do with that £44. Go to the cinema and have a burger? Put it towards a new bike? Take taxis instead of the bus when the shopping is heavy? As for the dog food, make them write to the manufacturer to ask more about what makes it different. Buy one can and try it out in a blind test on the dog. Whatever. But bring intelligence into play, because where intelligence comes in, the power of advertising withers. Expose rackets: show them pictures in the business section of the wealthy men and pretentious designers who are raking in your hard-earned money and spending it on persuading you to spend even more.

This applies even more when the pestering is for something the child itself wants. Even four-year-olds today have been known to pester for the right designer labels; it is nothing unusual for parents to spend £80 on a pair of trainers for a child whose feet are still growing two sizes a year. Parents in a recent survey admitted to running up debts to buy these things, pleading the guilt of being a working mother, or a single parent. At this point I curb my tongue, and refrain from the Rottweiler-journalism technique of suggesting that some people are such wimps they oughtn't to have children at all, and that governments should enforce a pre-conceptual test as to whether you can say Boo! to a goose. Instead, let me be helpful.

Here is a great truth: you do not have to let your children turn into mindless, grasping, boring little consumers. A baby is not born with the word 'Reebok' stamped on its heart. It wants colour and movement and interest and not labels. The things which turn children into mindless, grasping, boring etceteras are a) television and b) peer pressure. The cure for a) is to stop television becoming the centre of their lives. Encourage them to criticize it, analyse the commercials and why they are appealing, make up their own advertisements and take the mickey out of them. Offer alternatives: read books with them, travel, talk, dig a hole in the garden, build a card house. The only reason adolescent children get so addicted to television is that their lives are so narrow otherwise. And any parent who can afford £170 for a designer jacket can afford books, theatres, a trip up a mountain or on a canal. The credit card is the lazy way out: yes, even for the weekend-access father.

As for b), peer pressure is indeed painful, but children who suffer from it most are those who feel insecure anyway – either through home troubles or through being nagged too much. They can't buy friends anyway, poor little rats: the popular child in a class is very, very rarely the one with the newest tracksuit or most expensive fancy pen. It is the most alert, happy and confident one.

Be honest about the family budget: show it to them as they get older. Give teenagers – even bright eleven-year-olds – a clothes allowance to cover non-essentials like T-shirts, and make them stick to it. As they get older, encourage paper rounds and babysitting; offer to give up having a cleaner and pay the children instead for the same standard of work. Bring the children, in other words, into the real world of financial decisions. Divert that pester-energy into real thought and effort.

Supporting the family

If one partner is singlehandedly supporting the other, and the children, or merely earning much more, it should be made clear – out loud and as often as necessary – that they are happy, indeed honoured, to be doing so; and that neither of you values the other, as the world does, by the bank balance; and that everyone understands that there are other kinds of contribution to the world's wellbeing than the kinds which attract a salary. It is easier to think this way once you have children, because a baby has no bank balance at all and yet is the most precious person in the house: and children, fond though they get of money at certain phases, still instinctively value people for themselves, not their wealth or success. Call it a sentimental truism, but that attitude is the only thing which is going to get you through if – heaven forbid – you come to the crunch.

The crunch

We have just had a major world recession. As I write, it is said to be over; by the time this is published it could have started again. Certainly its effects will still be wiping out the finances of many families, often the kind who, until lately, thought themselves inviolable. That Victorian spectre, Ruin, has returned to haunt the 1990s. How families cope with it is a subject, to me, of undying fascination. Not least because, like many of the freelance middle-classes, I hourly expect it to happen to us.

There was a time when children's books were wonderful on the subject of financial ruin. Remember those bright, brave E. Nesbit mothers, like the one in *The Railway Children*? 'Now, my chickabiddies, we're going to have to play at being poor!' Remember how she gently broke the news that from now on it is 'Butter or jam, not both', while Daddy languished in prison over an obscure business injustice? Or think of The Wouldbegoods, the five Bastable children with their adventurous ploys for restoring their ruined father's fortunes. Or Sara Crewe in Frances Hodgson Burnett's *A Little Princess*, starving in her attic bedroom when her father's diamond mines went bust. Oh yes, those late Victorian children's authors knew how to twist the financial knife all right. But their characters were always troupers, and bankruptcy was just another big family adventure, the ultimate challenge to industry and optimism.

If modern children's writers know what's good for them, they will even now be working on modern plots involving the themes of ruin and repossession. Hundreds of families who once thought themselves to be inviolable are now going down the tube. They, along with all the plain and prudent people, are suffering from Europe's worst financial crisis since the war. The crisis, especially in Britain, is made worse by social trends because, after all, no family financial crisis is too extreme if you can stay put in the same house. But the rise of property-owning families (in the 1930s only fifteen percent of Britons owned their homes – now it is four times that) means that your home often vanishes with your prosperity. And the 1980s rush to independent schools means that children face a change of both school and friends when the money runs out. Those are British trends: but all over Europe rising standards of living have meant far more consumer comfort taken for granted; far more to kiss goodbye to when you can't keep up the payments.

So how is it, when families face the Crunch? How do relationships adjust to it? Do marriages break down (the evidence so far is yes, but fewer than you would think, and often by way of curious armed truces in which couples stay under the same roof because they can't sell it). But marriages which break down under financial disaster are in a way the least interesting. What has fascinated me for ages, and led me to poke my nose into a lot of families, is the way in which they manage to survive, and even flourish, in the areas which ultimately matter – even through bankruptcy.

So, since it has not actually happened to me yet, the best I can offer by way of advice is a plunge through some case histories, with the emphasis on survival as a family. Take Lizzie and Andrew Mills. Three years ago they each owned a Lamborghini, three of their children were at public school and they were joint directors of their company. A series of risky export deals landed them with bad debts; the bank lost its nerve and called in their loan. Andrew and Lizzie protested that they could only pay by selling part of the business, thus making the rest unprofitable. But the bank would not listen to their arguments, and within three months the company was in receivership, the London house sold at a knockdown price by order of the bank, and the family left shocked and bewildered in their former weekend cottage – luckily paid for with cash – with massive personal debts and no way of paying next term's school fees.

'Andrew collapsed,' says Lizzie. 'No other word for it. He felt it was his fault because he hadn't provided for his family. The company belonged to both of us and I was as much involved in the last disastrous decisions as he was, but some deep male thing took over and he blamed himself. Unfortunately, the side-effect was that he did damn all.'

It was Lizzie's arguments and manoeuvres which averted personal bankruptcy, her efforts which kept the family going over the next months. 'I cut up all the credit cards straight away and moved on to a cash economy. I took a night job as an office cleaner and a day job as a school cook.' She was overqualified for these jobs, but there was no time to look around: it was an emergency. Two of the children were very bright, and were offered scholarship bursaries by their schools, but the third decided to leave at sixteen. 'That,' say his parents, 'was the worst of it. Feeling that John had sacrificed his whole future because of us.' After prolonged lobbying by his father – who emerged from torpor to defend his son from what he saw as a disastrous decision – John agreed to enter the sixth form of his local comprehensive, which rather to his surprise he liked very much. 'I realized,' says Lizzie, 'that our preoccupation with private education had turned him into a bit of a snob. This has been good for him in the end.'

Weeks later, Andrew emerged properly from his depression, looked around and saw that Lizzie's energy had turned ruin into a perfectly bearable, if different, lifestyle. They are still paying off debts, but both are adamant that their relationship was never in real danger – partly because it was an established marriage of eighteen years, and partly because Lizzie in no way blamed her husband.

So compare that with the crunch faced by Teddy and Laura Enderby. In 1990 they were the model of a successful family: five years married, two beautiful children, a comfortable house, even a peacock on the lawn. They had a nanny, although Laura didn't work. Today, she lives with the children in a rented bungalow on a run-down estate, draws State benefits and does not know where Teddy is. She insists that the financial collapse was the whole reason for the split: 'He never told me it was coming – kept on spending money – then just came home and said "We've had it". He expected me to be the staunch little wife and say never mind, but I didn't. I threw things at him and told him he was a bastard and he had let us down.' This, perhaps, was not wise. He vanished, leaving her with all the difficulty and embarrassment of dealing with banks and bailiffs. His last words to her were 'I thought you'd understand, at least, but I suppose all you ever wanted was my money.' Laura wonders how a marriage could evaporate so fast, but when I told her about Lizzie Mills, she snorted. 'Oh, so boring, so tacky. Why should the woman hold the fort and clean offices while he nurses his pride and his so-called breakdown? Why shouldn't he clean bloody offices?'

But when she is tired and her guard slips, Laura sounds like a woman who wishes things had turned out differently. 'Well, OK, I was in shock. We might have worked something out.' But she knows that their marriage had been built on poor foundations: her mother had brought her up to think that if you were pretty and pleasant you would make a 'good' marriage, and get financial security and children. Her husband had learned to value himself by his earnings, and only to show emotion through giving gold bracelets rather than understanding. They lived amiably enough together as a family for as long as there was enough prosperity to give each of them space and prevent friction. Who knows how many other marriages are in this state, their ill-fitting cogs lubricated only by high earnings or solid capital?

A principle begins to emerge. Lizzie Mills worked it out: she says, 'You must not ever, ever, put too high a value on what you are losing. I cried over my big garden and the friends I couldn't afford to live near any more. But I could always see the wood for the trees. You have to think of money as rain: sometimes it showers down on you, sometimes it doesn't. It's nothing personal. You are the same person, it is the same marriage. I always knew that in the end we'd still be a family.'

Another principle seems to be that the younger the children, the less they actually mind. One pair said to their parents as soon as they heard the house was to go, 'Are you going to divorce?' They had enough friends, at six and eight, to know that these things happened. The moment they were assured that the family would stay together, even if it was in a tent, they were happy and co-operative and creative about it.

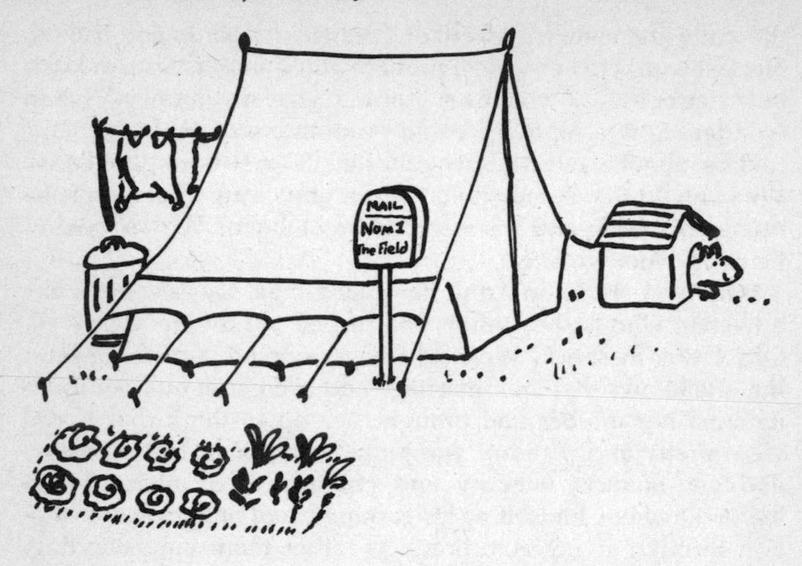

But another united family, with teenagers, found that a sudden drop in income hit their family life harder than they had expected. 'They were thirteen and fifteen,' says their mother, Erica. 'Still dependent financially, but wanting to feel independent. I never realized how much of their self-respect was paid for with money, and I deeply regret having let that happen. Emma had a horse, you see, and won cups at the Pony Club. John had a racing dinghy. The most painful scenes were about those things because, although we financed them and drove them around, they did belong to the children. They represented their greatest talents and greatest joys, and their common interests with their friends.' Horse and boat both had to go when the family moved to a small flat. Erica said, in fairness, that they could sell them and keep the money: 'But that rankled with me. I was keeping us all on £52 a week and taking in typing, and they suddenly got these windfalls of nearly £1,000 each. I resented it. They were so wrapped up in their own misfortunes they never suggested helping me at all.' Her mistake, she now says, was never having noticed that their interests were entirely dependent on expensive equipment. 'You just don't realize how much of modern social life and happiness hangs on money. A car, a boat, a caravan . . . all toys, but without them we snap.'

Perhaps that is the moral. You can always cope with a financial crunch provided you have not let money too far into your life in the first place. And provided that one of you has not valued him or herself – it usually seems to be a himself, but a woman can do it too – entirely in terms of what money they bring in to the family.

Several of the families I talked to, the Nouveau Ruined, were remarkably happy, giggly and full of jokes about their plight, real as it was. It would seem that there are temperaments and relationships which will always float above crisis, and perhaps we should all be working on developing that elusive, airy, bubble quality. And, as the saying goes, sit loose to comfort.

14: Fun, Fun, Fun: Trips and Treats, Guests and Gatherings

Family Time

As a natural hippie (oh, how I long to live in a commune, and only have to wipe down the kitchen table when it is my day for doing it, once a week), I used to set my face squarely against the ultra-cosiness of little nuclear families doing things together, without outsiders. Especially in matching sweaters. I wanted life to be diffuse, communard, free-flowing. 'The more the merrier!' I would cry, including hordes of other children in trips to steam fairs and seasides, filling the house with guests, idly offering the spare room to passers-by. It seemed, somehow, to dilute the fearful intensity of the early childraising years. So did the habit of taking private escapes – each parent away, with an adult friend, remembering how life used to be. I still do all these things, to some extent: but as children grow older, over eight anyway, it is increasingly borne in on me that parents and children need a ration of communal time, communal pleasures taken by all of them together and nobody else.

It is particularly true when both parents work. We have all got so efficient, so managerial about time-juggling in family life that we have created the curious phenomenon of the 'weatherhouse family'. This is the household in which one parent is always out while the other minds the children. The good side of this is that children get a chance to talk to each parent properly, without the parents lapsing into some sort of gibberish adult code which excludes them. The bad side is that if you are not careful, everyone's interests diverge so much that you are hardly a family at all, more like flatmates.

We have had periods like this, and my husband is particularly good at calling a halt to them and imposing family time. I will say 'Look, you take the children to the boat and I'll work –' and he will glare at me and say 'We'll all go'. And we do, and another shared memory, however trivial, ties us together.

It doesn't have to be an outing, or even a walk or a visit to the swimming pool. It could be just a family meal, after you have been eating separately for a while; a television programme or film everybody enjoys together, or a game of Scrabble or Monopoly. It could even be an accident: one family I know got stranded the other week in their boat, on a mudbank for eight hours with nothing to read or play with. They are, I would say, an averagely quarrelsome and difficult bunch, like any of us, but they rose to the occasion. They had a picnic-basket, plenty of beer and lemonade, and invented games like striking matches to draw charcoal pictures. They also, as the tide rose, sang their way through a whole songbook. They all agree, right down to the baby, that it was one of the best days out yet. Just being

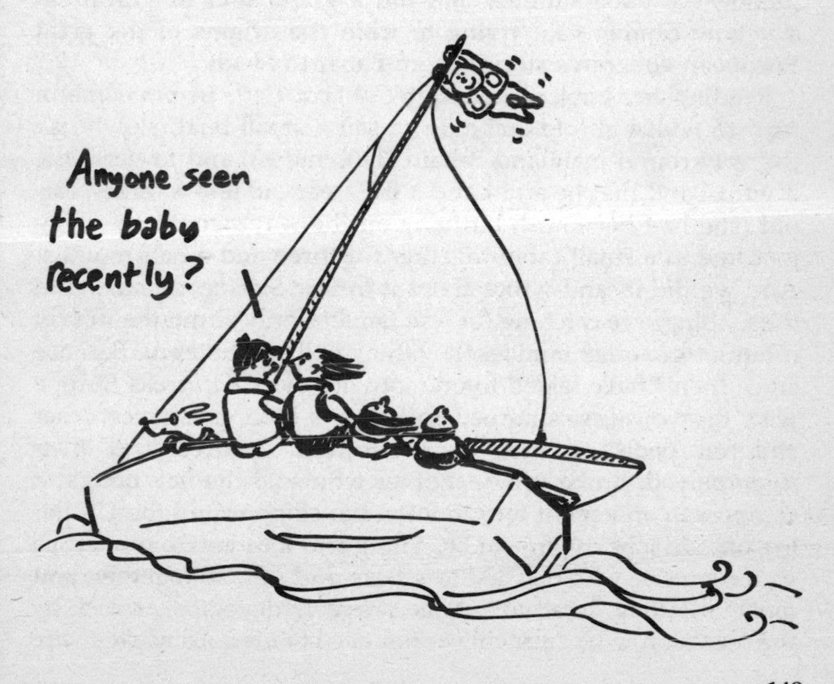

themselves, together, unable to get away, making the best of it. Every family needs a bit of this: if you don't get it, you feel the lack of it. It is worth forcing it even on your sulkiest, squeakiest wheel.

Adventures together

Adventures are something which sets off this family feeling, and makes it easier to recapture when you are all together for some later, minor thing like a meal or a walk. Some families plunge into really big adventures and weld themselves together that way. Years ago, the writer Christina Hardyment suddenly decided that she was tired of being a lackey and chauffeur, servicing children's clothes and delivering them to schools to be processed into adults. So she, and her whole family, removed themselves for a summer and did a grand tour of Europe in a yellow camper-van, trying to trace the origins of the great European children's stories, from Babar to Heidi.

Reading her book, *The Canary-Coloured Cart*, inspired me in turn to revive an old ambition to sail a small boat, slowly, all the way round mainland Britain (1700 miles), and to persuade my husband that he and I and a five-year-old and a three-year-old (she had her fourth birthday on the way) would get along just fine in a small cabin together for three and a half months. And we did it, and wrote about it in *One Summer's Grace*. And these things are catching (or else families only admit their crazy intentions to other families they think will understand). Because since then I have talked to one lot who bicycled across Europe with the youngest strapped to Father's bike, and three other children pedalling their own; to four children and their unemployed, broke, single mother who sold the flat, bought a campervan and spent four months travelling round the UK living off odd jobs, typing and cleaning and knitting; to numerous water-gypsies who decided to sell up and sail, all together; and most strikingly, to a workaholic property developer, struck by the recession, who suddenly announced to his gobsmacked wife and children that they were all going off for the whole summer to camp in the Rockies and see America, because business couldn't possibly be worse than it was and he wanted to get to know his children before it was too late.

All these trips were successes. Even one or two which were, technically, failures and did not reach their objective. The great pleasure of adventuring together is that however maddened you get (read *One Summer's Grace* if you want to know just how nasty a Mummy I can be), is that it lays down that set of common memories, family jokes, private language and general kinship which can be too quickly diffused and lost in the everyday modern world of TV and video, cars and hobbies and distant, centralized schools. A family adventure is a pressure-cooker, all right, but good nourishment comes out of it. A journey to a new place jolts you out of yourself, reinvigorates you, makes you see more clearly; if you all share this new vision, you grow closer together. The adventure can be quite small: one year after Christmas, feeling stale, we took the ferry across to France and the train to Paris, and stayed in an extremely cramped, extremely cheap hotel in Montmartre. All we did for two days was walk around: but adventures came our way. The children found gargoyles, and were spoken to kindly by a real Bishop. We saw a huge tent and discovered a temporary exhibition of Polish cribs. We ate different food. We climbed the Eiffel tower. Three years later, we all still talk about it: and it is all the better because we did it together. Even though there were at least five rows, numerous snapping-matches, and one child was in the process of coming down with a feverish 'flu. I am not sure we exactly enjoyed every minute at the time, and it was certainly not relaxing (I have never been so exhausted as on the ferry back). But we have enjoyed it a lot in retrospect, and retrospect lasts longer.

Holidays

Family holidays, ordinary ones, can do this. But the trouble is that we are all so tired by holiday time that we stop wanting adventures. So as a society we often opt for packaged relaxation: for places guaranteed to 'keep the kids busy all day long!' without parental intervention. We try to rule out adventure.

Work is partly at fault. There was an interesting survey recently which showed that whereas junior staff in companies – the fancy-free, childless ones – show no unwillingness to slope off on holiday as often as possible, senior staff (the kind with growing-up families or teenagers) often fail to take their full holiday entitlement, even when they are dispensable at work. I suspect that part of the reason, at least, is that the executives view a fortnight's trip away with their families as far more stressful than staying at work or having a bland week's rest at home. They have a point here: we are, in the majority of cases, talking about men, and it is an unfortunate quirk of fate and biology that just when a man gets to the stage of controlling a department full of bickering, unpredictable, backstabbing staff, his family life has matured as well – providing him with a parallel houseful of bickering, unpredictable, backstabbing teenagers. Taking this hornet's nest on holiday may seem to him every bit as stressful as staying put and masterminding a takeover bid for Amalgamated Consolidated Foodstuffs. You cannot, after all, sack your thirteen-year-old son.

Daddy, poor devil (or high-flying career Mummy), may have been working such long hours away from home, among professionals, that he/she has forgotten what it is to give a crisp order and have it met with indifference, derision, or a suggestion that he/she goes to get his/her own ice cream. By the time the whizzy parent has learned to wind down, to smile, to play beach-cricket and meet setbacks with a shrug, two upturned palms and a murmur of '*mañana*', the fortnight is up and it is time to go back to the office in a dangerously relaxed and vulnerable state, stripped of the protective carapace.

The answer to both problems – holiday stress and lack of family adventures – is, to me, the same. Be active. More research shows that professionals who actually do something with their families – hiking, sailing, cycling, camping – are far more willing to take the time off, and that families look forward to it more, and co-operate better, than if they were merely being hauled off to a predigested holiday experience which never quite lives up to its promise. For one thing, it forces everyone to concentrate, and therefore to make common purpose. The former BBC Director-General, Sir Ian Trethowan, used to say that only a sailing holiday really relaxed him because when he dropped the mooring he was forced to concentrate on the wind and tide instead of fretting about the latest BBC row. Even if the rest of the family merely wants to lounge around, while Mr or Ms Executive wants to chase about venting nervous energy, it can be organized. I met a very successful family boatload on a Greek flotilla once: Father had always wanted to sail, son wanted to chat up girls, and daughters and wife wanted a bikini holiday with lots of tavernas. Greek flotilla sailing being extremely undemanding, they all got what they wanted: Cap'n Bligh happy as Larry, commanded the ship, while the rest of them lay around getting brown and ignoring the commands.

If you have any of the outdoor urge (and I admit, some do not, and will be reading this section with shuddering loathing. Do yourself a favour. Pass on to the cultural section, will you?), you will find that it does a lot of good to family relationships if children can watch, and help, their parents struggling against the elements. We spent one Easter break living for three days in a horse-drawn caravan, huddling round fires of sticks in a bracing Norfolk gale, charring sausages and trying to remember which way to strap our stocky, wall-eyed mare into the shaft of the caravan for the next leg of the journey, up hill and down dale at 2 m.p.h. In the evenings we struggled with devilishly ingenious folding bunks, tucked up the under-sevens, and drank heavily to keep out the cold. Lots would be drawn last thing for who should squelch out to the meadow with a torch and check that the horse was still there. We never did manage to put up the fiendishly ingenious lavatory tent. All in all, it was a great success. As was the horrible Norfolk Broads cruiser in the sleet, and the canal-boat with ice on the windows and two lost lock-windlasses.

It is logical, I suppose. We are told that children need adult examples: they should see their parents facing difficulties and solving problems, so that they learn what work and life is all about. If they have a mother at home full-time, they see lots of shopping, cooking, bedmaking, gardening and so forth, and watch her facing up bravely to the business with the nit-comb, or the dog's mess on the carpet. But fathers – and working mothers – become enigmatic figures, who go off at dawn and come back exhausted at dusk. In between times they have done plenty of problem-solving, shown plenty of perseverance, but none of it to their children. In the old days children watched their fathers ploughing, and milking, and smithing, or running a shop; they copied them. No modern five-year-old is going to be thrilled by the tale of how Daddy carved up Rio Tinto Zinc today, or sold an insurance policy to an oil rig. And when holiday time comes, and both parents are clearly visible, what do they see? Mummy and Daddy queueing like sheep at airports, being shepherded around by air-hostesses and permed lady couriers, led on to coaches and delivered to the hotel like a load of washing. If it is a foreign holiday they see their parents not quite speaking the language, and being too debilitated by the heat even to make a decent sandcastle.

But if you run your own holiday – even if that just means reading the timetable and travelling independently – they see you grappling with problems (with luck, keeping your temper, too). Even in a twenty-mile seaside tailback in the car, your Dad is more likely to tell you rude jokes from his boyhood than he is on a bench at Heathrow airport. If you take a canal boat, or a horse-caravan, or hire a dinghy, children have to join in and be useful: throwing ropes ashore, holding the reins. Children are naturally busy and purposeful: it makes no sense to reduce them to beggars and drones, wheedling more money for theme park rides, hanging about waiting for the next meal or – if old enough – making sheep's eyes at Spanish waiters. Active holidays, in short, build character.

I liked to tell myself this at 2 a.m. in that appalling caravan, when I wanted a drink of water and found that although my ear was conveniently wedged against the caravan sink, the foot-pump was under my bunk, and the only way to it (without lifting the bunkboard and disturbing the rest) was to climb out over the shafts, on to the mud, heave myself up, wriggle into a narrow gap, crawl under the bunkboard and operate the pump by hand. When I got down there I remembered I had not put a glass under the tap. But it really built my character when I couldn't wriggle out without waking everyone. The children talk about it still. And about the night in the tent when Rose kicked the stopper out of the communal double Li-lo, and we all sank to the cold stony ground together. And the time she fell off the canal boat . . .

Cultural trips

Oh, all right. So you aren't an outdoor type, and the above accounts make you feel ill and tired before you even start. So stay in a hotel, or a villa, and go sightseeing. Before you swoon right away and say 'Whaddya mean, sightseeing? With children? All they want is a theme park!', let me assure you hand on heart that I know, I know. What you do is to promise them a theme park and do the other bit first. As in 'visiting-Paris-on-the-way-to-Eurodisney'. Believe me, keep at the sightseeing and in the end they will thank you for it. Well, they won't, but you will see the results, in their lives, of having been exposed to interesting things early on.

You may, however, have a few small frustrations along the way. I must have been ten years old when my mother took me to see the treasures of Tutankhamen. We were coming home by ship from South Africa, and took the option of leaving it at the southern end of the Suez Canal and rejoining in Port Said. I remember the Pyramids, and a Sphinx with no nose, and riding a camel called Monty. I remember our tour bus tearing through the desert towards the astonishing sight of our own ship apparently rolling through unbroken sands. I remember buying a riding-whip with a plastic head of Nefertiti for a handle. I do not, however, remember anything whatsoever about the treasures of Tutankhamen.

Years later, when they came to the British Museum in London, I mentioned at home that I was vaguely thinking of popping in to see them once the queues got shorter. My mother exploded. 'You've seen them! I took you! In Egypt!' It was the age-old cry of the culturally frustrated parent: you can take a child to wonders, but you can't make it think. Or even look. Some families give up, and say that you might as well stick to theme parks and paddling pools for smaller children, and disco joints and windsurf-hire beaches for teenagers. Some dump the children all day in a French-style 'Club Mickey' and go off alone to look at pictures and buildings. Sightseeing with children, they aver, is a waste of time. Venice is off, until they leave home.

But is it? Despite my total amnesia concerning the boy Pharaoh's tomb, I have perfectly clear memories of Monty the camel (his breath smelt), the Sphinx, the sand, and the crowds of Cairo. Delving into memories from years before, when I was only four years old in Thailand, I could draw you a clear picture right now of the huge toes of the Sleeping Buddha. I am not sure I ever managed the long walk to its head. I seem to remember something about wet knickers. And from almost babyhood, I remember the petrified figures of Pompeii sleeping eternally amazed in their coats of lava, even though I spent barely an hour in that museum. As for the cave in Switzerland where Saint Nicholas of Flue fled his family to lead a hermit life . . . well, obscure it may be, but I remember that, too. Possibly it was impressed on my mind by certain acrimonious parental discussions about men who are never there when you need them, always sloping off to the office, or cave . . . Ah well.

The moral seems to be that it is worth taking children to see the sights, wherever you are – as long as you don't expect them to see what you see. A childhood travelling the world because of my father's job has, at least, taught me that. Children, and teenagers, do not carry around the same cultural baggage as adults: they have to be allowed their own vision. They don't think 'Ooh! The Taj Mahal!' or 'Venice! How wonderful. What was it Ruskin said . . . ?' They just go round corners and see things, and say 'Oh, look!' Often they are actually looking in what we, who have read the guidebooks, regard as an inappropriate direction. Every parent knows the experience of taking a child to the zoo and finding it prefers the plastic frog-shaped wastepaper baskets to the real animals; we put up with that. So extend the same tolerance even when you have travelled hundreds of miles to introduce them to the marvels of civilization, and they end up mesmerized by a lizard on the castle wall.

You can manage, with superhuman effort, to prevent yourself from getting annoyed when a child stands before the finest stained-glass window in Europe and refuses to raise its eyes. You can tell yourself that children often spot far more interesting things, less obvious ones, and give the whole family a new perspective. They see a carved mouse on a knight's foot on a tomb, an unexpected eagle in a ruined mosaic floor, a gargoyle with its tongue out. So play along, and enjoy it. Forget the stained glass; they can get a postcard of that on the way out. The sure way of putting a child off travelling, and art, and civilization, for life is to insist in a shrill hysterical tone that it take a proper look at the marble Madonna or whatever, because it's all been paid for with good money. You can promise (and deliver) more physical, childish or teenage satisfactions later in the day or the week; you can make a game of it, as one family does, by letting everyone choose a postcard at the entrance to an art gallery, and then dash off and find the original, and scribble down all they can about it.

However, as any sweating family fighting its way through the Acropolis in August can tell you, there are ground rules. Duck out of the big crowds. There are always back streets, byways, lesser sights which are equally characteristic of a new city and

– to a child – different and impressive. If St Peter's Basilica is uncomfortably crowded, well, Rome has other wonderful churches. If the most famous and intricate of the Lycian rock tombs in southern Turkey seems to have six coaches at the foot of its steps, it is not far to a miraculously silent, equally ancient and atmospheric corner where there is a lesser tomb. Remember that if children are still shorter than adults, there is not much fun looking at anything through a forest of bottoms and dangling camcorders. Use bad weather, or early mornings, to see the big attractions.

Along the Turkish coast once, caught in some violent April rain, we took a bracing walk to a two-thousand-year-old ruined amphitheatre in a hillside. Nobody else was there. The rain stopped. We sat on the tiers of seats while the children, still under five, ran around at the bottom. Old pantomime aficionados that they were, they rapidly worked out that this must be a theatre. Immediately they put on an impromptu production, lasting five minutes, and ending in a spirited rendering of 'Wheel yer perambulator John, wheel it nice and slow!' The acoustics worked beautifully, as they always had; I like to think that they got the point of amphitheatres that day, and got it rather better than they would have done on a guided tour.

With older children, you can be more structured; but the trick, I fear, is to read the guidebook yourself before you go, mug up on all the history, and then keep quiet about it until the actual questions come. If someone looks at a castle and says 'How old is that? Who built it?' it is nice to have an answer. But nothing is more deadening than the educational parent who never lets up.

As for museums, remember only that if you don't force them on children, antiquity and natural history fascinate quite naturally. A museum does not need to be a theme-parky, interactive 'experience', filled with novelty heritage waxworks or clockwork knights. These are all good fun as far as they go, but even the most conventional museums can thrill children who are relaxed and receptive (because their companions are). I recently helped escort a school trip round the Natural History Museum in

London – ten- and eleven-year-olds – and while they liked the obvious show-stoppers like the interactive rooms and the giant Blue Whale, on the bus home they talked with equal affection about the enormous Victorian cases of stuffed hummingbirds, and some rather dry-looking but ancient fossils. A skeleton, of course, is always very welcome to all ages; and so is a relief map with tiny mountains, or any kind of stuffed furry animal. Actually, so are the hot-air grilles which blow your coat up over your head; the trick is not to get irritated when your family seems to find these more riveting than the exhibits. You can't sop up wisdom all day, can you? If adults are allowed to flirt in gondolas, children should be free to play on hot-air grids.

It is worth persevering, through all the low moments, the whining for ice cream in the Uffizi and lavatories on the Rialto. When things get desperate, dive for a cafe. When children whine, don't whine back. Uplift the atmosphere. Jump on a wall. Act childish and enthusiastic yourself. Anything which sticks, any wonder of the world, is a massive investment in their mental and spiritual future. We spend spare money on travel, always, rather than on dressing respectably or furnishing the house like grown-ups should, so we have taken the children to quite a few places. After journeys round Britain, through southern Turkey and Greece and a few jaunts elsewhere in Europe, I consulted them as to their best memories. 'Center Parcs,' they said, and as my face fell, 'and lovely carved holes in Turkey where they used to put dead bodies, and Notre Dame in Paris, and the cafe in Greece with a roof made of leaves. And the log-ride at Pleasurewood Hills Theme Park. And going up through clouds in the dark on the cable-car to the Allmenalp. And landing on Orkney and finding the puppet workshop.' A mixed bag. I was content.

However, I also cherish the wise remark of a fellow-journalist criticizing over-purposefulness on family holidays. It was important, she said, to remember that a vital part of holidays, for bigger children and adolescents, was 'lying upside-down on a bunk bed while it rains outside, trying to follow the instructions in a dog-eared book of magic tricks.' Don't try too hard . . .

Going on Holiday with Other Families

This does not invalidate all the above family bonding: it can actually improve it, provided you are really friends and have roughly the same ideas about domestic squalor, money, bedtimes, discipline, and what constitutes bad language in the young. A modicum of family privacy helps. So does a case or two of wine. However, two points: a) try it out on a weekend or two first, preferably under stressful conditions like a hire-boat, and b) make a firm pact that all parents are allowed to shout at all children, whether related or not, for any misbehaviour. Half-way down the case of wine, it becomes quite difficult to remember which of these children are yours anyway. If, that is, the holiday is going well.

Tribal Gatherings

An alarmingly huge version of family bonding sessions. Britain was highly entertained last Easter, and many echoes raised, by an enterprising reporter's group photograph of the Health Secretary, Virginia Bottomley, and forty-odd relations of all possible ages striding out across the Isle of Wight in chunky sweaters for their traditional Easter Monday all-weather tribal walk. They sang, if reports be accurate, Rolf Harris's 'Two Little Boys', then gathered around an old windmill while an uncle imparted heroism to a new generation – some of it still in baby-buggies – by re-telling the stories of Captain Scott and the loss of the *Titanic*. These had, apparently, been told first at the time they were hot news, and ever since, each year, the Garnett clan assemble to tell them again.

There was also some kind of ritual surrounding a fountain-pen lost in 1918, but the family quite properly keeps the details to itself.

They got guyed for this excursion in certain public prints, with the words 'wholesome', 'clean', and 'Enid Blyton' being used in the authentic thin, sour tones of 1990s journalism as expressions of extreme disdain. But I think the clan Garnett/Bottomley are on to something here. In an age when 'relationships' are more popular than relations, the rest of us might pick up a few useful post-modern tips from them. The event has been going on for eighty-nine years in the Garnett family, and is probably the best insurance the Minister has of not turning into the kind of arrogant monster so many politicians make of themselves. Mrs Bottomley was the one accosted by the reporters, but their emphasis was clearly all wrong. Anyone who knows anything about large families will realize that it is most unlikely that she would have been the natural spokesman. Once sucked into a huge tribal gathering, she would revert to being someone's sister, someone's niece, just another listener in the respectful crowd round the uncle who for some mysterious family reason was top-dog at the time and got to tell the stories. She was just another comparative junior, knowing her place.

One of the great merits of family gatherings is the way the pecking-order imposed by the outside world (You Cabinet Minister, me nonentity) counts for nothing once the family drawbridge is up. Cousins, still less siblings, are no respecters of persons. They know too much about your calf loves and acne. Taken in the right spirit, this is not only very good for the soul of the Cabinet Minister, film star or tycoon but provides reassurance for the rest of the family. There is nothing quite like an unimpressed auntie ('Nasty common skirt, dear, and you're looking pasty') to pull an international superstar down to size.

The second useful example set by the Garnett tribe is that they hold this event on a regular but unmomentous day. Big family gatherings get a bad name because most families only assemble *en masse* for funerals (sad, low-key, with the threat of a contentious will in the offing), weddings (where there is always a comparatively strange family present to inhibit everyone), or Christmas (where someone is fed up with cooking and the children are out of control). In our family we occasionally hold what is known as a Counting, after the Counting of the Family in Stella Gibbons' *Cold Comfort Farm*. 'We'm violent folk, we Starkadders. Some on us pushes others down wells. Others die o' drink or goes mad. 'Tes difficult to keep count on us, so once a year Grandmother she holds a gatherin', and she counts us all to see how many on us 'as died in th' year.' My mother excels in the role of Aunt Ada Doom, and it is observable that these gatherings – ideally four siblings, a cousin if available, partners and children and the odd terrified in-law or house guest – work best when they occur for no particular reason. They might be even better if built around an absurdity, like a wet picnic and a hunt for a 75-year-old fountain pen. The strain would be off.

But the main Garnett lesson is one of sheer scale. When people shrink away from the idea of a family gathering, they are not really thinking of great festivals like this. The really hellish family gatherings are the small claustrophobic ones: the kind where parents fuss over adult children through an endless Easter weekend, where social differences arise with new daughters-in-law, or one distant, depressing relation comes on a duty visit to a tight and nervy nuclear family. Avoid these by all means: but foster instead the huge, momentous tribal rally. Every child has a right to have an Aunt Ada Doom smelling of mothballs and cursing in black; to hear antique feuds creaking back into life, to be told the terrible tale of Uncle Walter and to discover how strangely like him (or her) his cousins look. Multi-generation gatherings are the best history lesson that school can never provide.

Never mind if they are not pure pleasure. Remember Amos in *Cold Comfort Farm*: 'He liked to have his kith about him. Although of course, he never said so, or cheered up when they were.' There are, however, one or two pointers for families which find themselves (usually by owning the largest room) the hosts of family gatherings:

- **Never compete.** It does not matter that your mother, or mother-in-law, always has four courses at Christmas dinner, home-made nibbles and everyone in their best dress. Do it your way, the way that you can cope with.

Feed people what is reasonably easy, or what someone else in the family can help with. And smile, and lubricate everyone with drinks and jokes. I find paper streamers and cardboard balancing butterflies hurled all over a table distract people wonderfully from the non-matching cutlery and plates. The prevailing dodginess of cooking and presentation can be driven right out of everyone's mind by the simple (now traditional) expedient of concluding the pudding course with those dreadful indoor fireworks, with a succession of tipsily lit coloured mini-volcanoes culminating in the Giant Serpent which shoots out of its black tablet in the most obscene fashion. The reek of cordite will forever be associated in the various cousins' minds with Auntie Libby and Uncle Paul going a bit manic again.

- **Never apologize.** The point of coming together as an extended family is to see one another, and reminisce, and get a good look at how big the cousins have grown. If, for uncontrollable reasons, the barbecue food is a bit burnt or the plaster has come down from the ceiling two days before and made everything white, it does not matter. My mother, whose youth was colourfully well-travelled, always helpfully says, 'Imagine you are all in the ruins of Warsaw. This would be luxury.' So have low standards. Frankly, if any of the cousins are under seven, they will lower them anyway before you know where you are.
- **Be a UN Peacekeeping Force** if you have to. Only don't be afraid to show the warring factions your heavy artillery. If someone threatens to ruin the gathering by dredging up some dreary family quarrel over religion, inheritance, or who stole whose toy train in 1952, raise your voice commandingly and say, 'I will not have ill-feeling over my table at Christmas/Easter/a family party. It is a bad example to the children. Peace and goodwill to all men. Thank you.' The trick is to take precisely the same tone with everyone, whether it is Great-Granny or the new toddler or your spouse or child. It works surprisingly well, provided you don't burst into tears.

- **Grow up.** Someone has to. The trouble with tribal gatherings is that siblings, when they meet thirty years later, always revert to the age of about six for a while. Big brothers start teasing, little sisters taking offence, mothers bossing their grown daughters and fussing over sons who are forty-three, for heaven's sake. This is not a Freudian therapy session or a rebirthing process, it is a lunch party or a family walk. Unresolved family conflicts can damn well stay unresolved. Unless you are prepared to whirl round and confront them with fearless openness, one-to-one in a corner of the kitchen, as in, 'Look, Nigel, I know I let your white mice die while you were away at boarding-school, but they would be dead now anyway, and you are a Bishop now, so I think you ought to forgive me.'

The family year

The family year needs milestones: something on the calendar to look forward to. You can justify them by saying they represent cultural heritage, or religious faith, or you can just take them as a bit of fun, especially at the duller times of year. We have celebrated, in our time, not only all four birthdays and Christmas but New Year, Epiphany, Pancake Day, Easter, Harvest Supper, Hallowe'en, Guy Fawkes, May Day, St Nicholas' day, and Pudding Thursday (a bit obscure that, but all you need do is eat Yorkshire pudding). Give me time and I shall devise ways of marking Shakespeare's birthday, Michaelmas, Midsummer's Eve, St Andrew's Day, St Patrick's Day (for the Scottish and Irish connection) and if any Americans should drop in I will include Thanksgiving and Groundhog Day with pleasure. On discovering that April 14th used to be celebrated as First Cuckoo Day, I seriously considered a Cuckoo cake, a Cuckoo race, a Cuckoo-imitating competition . . . anything. Last Comic Relief charity day, we organized a sponsored Filth-a-thon (get as filthy as you can in five minutes, mud and paint and flour provided,

Polaroids taken) and to my slight horror I now find that this is now considered to be an annual event. 'At next year's, we could have jam to smear on our hair, as well . . .'

Celebrating does not have to be expensive: a paper flag or two to paint, a meal around the table, a game if you can. Some families make beautiful things, blow their own Easter eggs and paint gorgeous scenes on them, build their own flower garlands, crystallize violets and cook marvellous traditional dishes. Others, more like us, go for the broad sweep, and merely haul out the candlesticks, the paper butterflies and the fancy napkins, wind up the collection of tinplate toys to give a festive air, and haul in a couple of other families to have an egg-hunt, or an Epiphany cake with a bean in it and paper crown for the bean-finder. Family and neighbourhood celebrations should be relaxed, and if you are so cack-fisted that relaxed equals shoddy (blown eggs cracked and mended with Sellotape), so what? Colour and celebration matter more than arts and crafts in this context. If you devise a family year that everyone likes, early on, you will find to your infinite, touched, sentimental joy that even huge hulking teenagers with safety-pins in their noses and luminous hair will suddenly say, 'Hey, where's the wax Easter lamb? We always have it out!' Aaaah.

House guests and sleepovers

Oh, I do love a houseful. It is such a marvellous excuse to let standards slip even further than usual. My happiest weekends at home have been spent with visiting families of six all laid out like sardines, head-to-tail in sleeping bags on a heap of cushions. It must be admitted that my husband does not feel quite the same about this matter, but if sufficiently lubricated, he gets by. The children love it, too. Lots and lots of people to play cricket with! Visiting babies to show off to! One or two suggestions, though, from bitter experience:

- **Respect children's territory.** In some households, it is customary for one child at least to be regularly ousted from their bedroom when visitors come, thus enabling the visitor to sleep in a choo-choo train bed, under posters of Jason Donovan and with a plentiful reading supply of Star Trek annuals by the bed. Fine. But if you happen to have the kind of child who feels passionately about territory, forget it. It is not worth risking the fuming atmosphere. To put the guest on a camp bed in the sitting-room would be much, much better all round. Or move out of your own room, if you like. Sometimes, of course, children can be persuaded by various means to give up their rooms: but you run the risk of them glaring at the guest half-way through the weekend with 'My Mummy had to pay me £3 to let you have my bed'.
- **Sharing with visiting children** or cousins they do not know is equally fraught. Whereas most children of all ages adore having their own friends share their room, alien children – perhaps with funny habits, like folding their clothes – can be worrying. They might snore. You could try persuading your reluctant sharer, but a better way is massive bribery of an imaginative nature. As in 'It'll be like a party. When you wake up in the morning, if you creep downstairs together you'll find a special breakfast. But you'll have to look for it. There are rhyming clues all over the ground floor of the house.' Then you, and the visiting parents, get quietly pie-eyed and make up the rhyming clues late at night. You can offer further inducements if the children are quiet enough not to wake you up.
- **It is a special occasion.** Spoiling is OK. One night, a visiting nine-year-old without parents present got so upset and wailing that I decided on even more extreme bribery. After trying repeatedly to calm him down, with the help of his big brother, I went in, switched on the light and said, 'Charles. We can do two things. Either I can get dressed and drive you home to your mother, which is boring. Or you can shut up, not make another sound, and

when you wake up in the morning there will be a mystery present on your pillow and everyone else's pillow,' (one always has a stock of mystery presents, does one not? Surely!) Within ten minutes everyone was asleep, including me. What the child was upset about, or pretending to be upset about, we never found out, really. But my instinct that it can't have been much was triumphantly vindicated . . .

- **Keep hospitality simple.** It is tempting to plunge into the world of home-made croissants and designer food, especially if long-lost friends or distant family have come on a rare visit. Don't. Unless your teenagers are old enough to make a lot of it. As the Bible almost says, better a dinner of herbs where love is, than a stalled ox-and-a-lot-of-histrionics-about-the-gravy therewith.
- **Give single people space.** Friends with children, especially small children, are usually so grateful to have their entire family absorbed into your household for the weekend that they fall in happily with anything you are doing. Even going down to someone else's supermarket instead of your own is a pleasant holiday. But childless guests – it is easy to forget – can be easily overwhelmed by family life. In a

family, you become so accustomed to constant company of whatever age that you hardly notice it any more. What to you might seem a pleasant, good-tempered susurration of youthful chat could sound like a bloody awful racket to an ageing great-uncle, or nervy career girl trying to brood about her latest man. As I am always pointing out how wonderful single friends are for families to have, how liberating and amusing and generally nice-to-know, it is worth putting some thought into not driving them crazy when they do come round. How you do it depends on your own habits, house and family timetable. But think about it.

- **Don't try to show off your perfect family.** This will only annoy everybody: those with families of their own, and those without. Do not make children of any age perform unless they want to, whether their forté is the cello or tap-dancing. And however hard it is to be natural under the scrutiny of outsiders – and one learns a great deal about people's family life by staying with them, else where would I have got material for much of this book? – try to act the way you normally would. Particularly with younger children, be yourself: shout where you would shout, cajole and cuddle where you would cajole and cuddle. Otherwise a strange, false, tense atmosphere will build up. Of course older children and teenagers have to learn the idea of 'company manners' and making outsiders feel comfortable. But even they should not be expected to change every single aspect of their behaviour for visitors. If it is that bad, perhaps they should be changing it full-time . . .

15: Grumbles and Celebrations: Words on Family Life

The last thing I want to do, coming to the end of this book, is conclude it roundly, or offer any trite summing-up of family life. Each family is different, every year in its life is different, and above all every age is different. Society, economics and the climate of opinion all change. There is no point looking back to any 'golden age' of family management; there is no template for an ideal home life. All we have is the most basic rules of all: about kindness, fairness and chivalry towards one another's weaknesses.

So let us end with diverse voices from the past: grumbling about, celebrating or mocking this great institution. And listen for the echoes: for those central things which never, thank goodness, do change.

> Thy wife shall be as a fruitful vine by the sides of thine house; thy children like olive plants round about thy table.
>
> *Psalm 128*

> *A Respectable Family taking the air*
> *Is a subject on which I could dwell;*
> *It contains all the morals that ever there were,*
> *And it sets an example as well.*
>
> HILAIRE BELLOC, *A Moral Alphabet*

> Whoever considers the length and feebleness of human infancy, with the concern which both sexes naturally have for their offspring, will easily perceive that there must be a union of male and female for the education of the young, and that this union must be of considerable duration.
>
> DAVID HUME, *A Treatise of Human Nature*, 1740

That all men should be brothers is the dream of people who have no brothers.

CHARLES CHINCOLLES, *Pensées de Tout le Monde*

You are the bows from which your children as living arrows are sent forth.

KAHLIL GIBRAN, *The Prophet*, 1923

'Like as the arrows in the hand of the giant, even so are the young children' – so says the excellent office in our Prayer-book appointed for the churching of women. 'Happy is the man that hath his quiver full of them.' So say I: but then, don't let him discharge his quiver upon us that are weaponless . . .

I know there is a proverb, 'Love me, love my dog'; that is not always so very practicable, particularly if the dog be set upon you to tease you or snap at you in sport. But a dog, or a lesser thing – any inanimate substance, as a keepsake, a watch or a ring, a tree, or the place where we last parted when my friend went away on a long absence, I can make shift to love, because I love him, and anything that reminds me of him; provided it be in its nature indifferent, and apt to receive whatever hue fancy can give it. But children have a real character and an essential being of themselves: they are amiable or unamiable *per se*; I must love them or hate them as I see cause for either in their qualities. A child's nature is too serious a thing to admit of its being regarded as a mere appendage to another human being, and to be loved or hated accordingly. They stand with me upon their own stock, as much as men and women do.

CHARLES LAMB, *Essays of Elia*, 1823

The family is a court of justice which never shuts down for night or day.

MALCOLM DE CHAZAL

Every large family has its angel and its demon

JOSEPH ROUX, *Meditations of a Parish Priest*

'Accidents will occur in the best-regulated families; and in families not regulated by that pervading influence which sanctifies while it enhances the – a – I would say, in short, by the influence of a Woman, in the lofty character of Wife, they may be expected with confidence, and must be borne with philosophy.'

MR MICAWBER in *David Copperfield*, 1850, Charles Dickens

'I have known him [Micawber] come home to supper with a flood of tears, and a declaration that nothing was now left but a jail; and go to bed making a calculation of the expense of putting bow-windows in the house "in case anything turned up", which was his favourite expression.'

MRS MICAWBER, *ibid*

I was never of opinion, that the honest man who married and brought up a large family, did more service than he who continued single and only talked of population.

OLIVER GOLDSMITH, *The Vicar of Wakefield*, 1766

There is a photograph in existence of Aunt Sadie and her six children sitting round the tea-table at Alconleigh. The table is situated, as it was, is now, and ever shall be, in the hall, in front of a huge open fire of logs . . .

The other children, between Louisa's eleven and Matt's two years, sit round the table in party dresses or frilly bibs, holding cups or mugs according to age, all of them gazing at the camera with large eyes opened wide by the flash, and all looking as if butter would not melt in their round pursed-up mouths. There they are, held like flies in the amber of that moment – click goes the camera and on goes life; the minutes, the days, the years, the decades, taking them further and further from that happiness and promise of youth, from the hopes Aunt Sadie must have had for them, and from the dreams they dreamed for themselves. I often think there is nothing quite so poignantly sad as old family groups.

NANCY MITFORD, *The Pursuit of Love*, 1945

Children begin by loving their parents; as they grow older they judge them; sometimes they forgive them.

OSCAR WILDE, *The Picture of Dorian Gray*, 1891

'An unhappy alternative is before you, Elizabeth. From this day you must be a stranger to one of your parents. – Your mother will never see you again if you do *not* marry Mr Collins, and I will never see you again if you *do*.'

MR BENNET in *Pride and Prejudice*, 1813, Jane Austen

Boys will be boys – and even that wouldn't matter if we could only prevent girls from being girls.

ANTHONY HOPE HAWKINS, 1900

The tiger on the other hand, is kittenish and mild
He makes a pretty playfellow for any little child;
Mothers of large families, who claim to common sense
Will find a Tiger well repays the trouble and expense . . .

HILAIRE BELLOC, *The Bad Child's Book of Beasts*, 1896

Judith's breath came in long shudders. She thrust her arms deeper into her shawl. The porridge gave an ominous leering heave; it might almost have been endowed with life, so uncannily did its movements keep pace with the human passions that throbbed above it.

'Cur!' said Judith levelly, at last. 'Coward! Liar! Libertine! Who were you with last night? Moll at the mill or Violet at the vicarage? Or Ivy, perhaps, at the ironmongery? Seth – my son. . . .' Her deep, dry voice quivered, but she whipped it back, and her next words flew out at him like a lash.

'Do you want to break my heart?'

'Yes' said Seth, with an elemental simplicity.

The porridge boiled over.

STELLA GIBBONS, *Cold Comfort Farm*

Every generation revolts against its fathers and makes friends with its grandfathers.

LEWIS MUMFORD, 1931

The family! . . . that dear octopus from whose tentacles we never quite escape, nor in our innermost hearts ever quite wish to . . .

DODIE SMITH, *Dear Octopus*

The best way to keep children home is to make the home atmosphere pleasant – and let the air out of the tyres.

DOROTHY PARKER (1893–1967)

Far from being the basis of the good society, the family, with its narrow privacy and tawdry secrets, is the source of all our discontents.

SIR EDMUND LEACH, BBC Reith Lecture, 1967

Gordon grew up in the atmosphere of cut-down clothes and stewed neck of mutton. His father, like the other Comstocks, was a depressed and therefore depressing person, but he had some brains and slight literary turn. And seeing that his mind was of the literary type and he had a shrinking horror of anything to do with figures, it had seemed only natural to Gran'pa Comstock to make him into a chartered accountant . . .

Gordon was sent to wretched, pretentious schools whose fees were around £120 a year. Even these fees, of course, meant fearful sacrifices at home. Meanwhile Julia, who was five years older than he, received as nearly as possible no education. She was, indeed, sent to one or two poor, dingy little boarding schools, but she was taken away for good when she was sixteen. Gordon was 'The boy' and Julia was 'the girl' and it seemed natural to everyone that 'the girl' should be sacrificed to 'the boy'. Moreover, it had early been decided in the family that Gordon was 'clever'. Gordon, with his wonderful 'cleverness', was to win scholarships, make a brilliant success in life, and retrieve the family fortunes – that was the theory, and no one believed in it more firmly than Julia.

GEORGE ORWELL, *Keep the Aspidistra Flying*, 1936

My father was frightened of his mother, I was frightened of my father, and I am damned well going to make sure that my children are frightened of me.

GEORGE V (1865–1936)

Parents learn a lot from their children about coping with life.

MURIEL SPARK (*b.* 1918)

Children aren't happy with nothing to ignore
And that's what parents were created for

OGDEN NASH (1902–71)

Some nieces won't, some nieces can't
Imbibe instruction from an aunt . . .

A.E. HOUSMAN (1859–1936)

All happy families resemble each other, each unhappy family is unhappy in its own way.

LEO TOLSTOY, *Anna Karenina*, 1875–7

The thing that impresses me most about America is the way parents obey their children.

THE DUKE OF WINDSOR (1894–1972)

Insanity is Hereditary: you get it from your kids.

SAM LEVENSON

When I was a boy of fourteen, my father was so ignorant I could hardly stand to have the old man around. But when I got to be twenty-one, I was astonished at how much he had learned in seven years.

MARK TWAIN (1835–1910)

A husband should not insult his wife publicly, at parties. he should insult her in the privacy of the home.

JAMES THURBER (1894–1961)

It must have been some unmarried fool that said 'A child can ask questions that a wise man cannot answer' because, in any decent house, a brat that starts asking questions is promptly packed off to bed.

ARTHUR BINSTEAD, journalist (1861–1914)

The first half of our lives is ruined by our parents, and the second by our children.

CLARENCE DARROW, US attorney (1857–1938)

The family! Home of all social evils, a charitable institution for indolent women, a prison workshop for the slaving breadwinner and a hell for children.

AUGUST STRINDBERG (1849–1912)

One would be in less danger
From the wiles of the stranger
If one's own kin and kith
Were more fun to be with . . .

OGDEN NASH (1902–71)

The family is one of nature's masterpieces.

GEORGE SANTAYANA, *The Life of Reason*, 1905–6

Index

How *Not* to Be a Perfect Mother

Libby Purves

Perfect Mothers:
smile serenely
run immaculate homes
make nappies into kites
read books on Child Development
never raise their voices

Real Mothers:
have food on their jumpers
never finish anything
limp from treading on Sticklebricks
read romantic novels on the quiet
squeak with exhaustion

With sparkling humour and a low cunning born of four years spent catching food before it hits the floor, Libby Purves shows that even the most unpromising madonna can survive the years of looking after babies and toddlers.

Drawing on her own experience of domestic havoc with two babies, and on the wit and wisdom of fifty like-minded mothers, Libby Purves shamelessly describes how to cut the corners and bend the rules which never mattered much anyway.

An invaluable guide to being an imperfect mother and enjoying it.

How Not to Raise a Perfect Child

Libby Purves

Which is yours?

A Perfect Child:
Neatly dressed and practising the violin before breakfast
Top of the class and captain of everything
Unfailingly obedient and sweet-tempered
The obvious product of a perfect mother

A Real Child:
Prefers shoelaces undone and shirt untucked
Shouts 'Bum!' at Granny
Hates your best friend's children
The normal offspring of imperfect parents

With the same wit and understanding that made *How Not to be a Perfect Mother* an international bestseller, Libby Purves now turns her attention to the next phase of motherhood: from three to eight years old. Some problems – nappies, flying food, and tiny heads jammed into saucepans – have certainly disappeared, but entirely new ones have emerged: playgroup days, school beginnings, corrosive Mum-upmanship, impossible questions, rude words, early friendships . . .

Her incredulous eye for detail and affectionate lack of illusion have resulted again in a resoundingly practical and compassionate guide: a realistic celebration of family life from pets to party hats, classrooms to casualty wards. Above all, it is a reassuring reminder that there is no such thing as a perfect child, any more than there was ever a perfect mother.